MAKING LIFE COUNT

LESTER SUMRALL
FRANK SUMRALL
PETER SUMRALL
STEVE SUMRALL

Thomas Nelson Publishers
Nashville • Camden • New York

Published in Nashville, Tennessee, by Thomas Nelson, Inc., Publishers, and distributed in Canada by Lawson Falle, Ltd., Cambridge, Ontario.

Printed in the United States of America.

Unless otherwise indicated, Scripture quotations are from THE NEW KING JAMES VERSION of the Bible, © 1979, 1980, 1982, Thomas Nelson, Inc., Publishers.

Scripture references marked KJV refer to the King James Version of the Bible.

Scripture references marked AMP are from The Amplified Bible: Old Testament, copyright © 1962, 1964 by Zondervan Publishing House and are used by permission.

Scripture references marked TLB are from The Living Bible (Wheaton, Illinois: Tyndale House Publishers, 1971) and are used by permission.

Library of Congress Cataloging in Publication Data
Main entry under title:

Making life count.

1. Christian life—1960-   —Addresses, essays, lectures. I. Sumrall, Lester Frank, 1913-
I. Sumrall, Lester Frank, 1913-
BV4501.2.M3297   1985   248.4   85-10624
ISBN 0-8407-5988-6

Contents

Preface

An inspirational handbook of essays on how to make the most of your life, *Making Life Count* consists of ten lessons in values and Christian living. In a lucid, practical style, Dr. Sumrall and his sons, Frank, Steve, and Peter, present information on how to find and personify God's will. The book is structured so that each lesson builds on the ones preceding, and each paves the way for the one that follows.

The essays contain basic instruction in Christian beliefs as well as advice; thus, the first three lessons deal with matters that are of concern to Christians of all ages, especially "spiritual children," those who are new in the Spirit. Throughout, the emphasis is on basic Christian values and priorities.

Chapters 4 through 8 discuss matters of concern to "spiritual adults," who are often under pressure from a variety of sources. "How to Achieve Your Potential" and "How to Stand Tall" emphasize attaining the self-knowledge and self-respect that lead to personal fulfillment and Christian growth. "How to Love" and "How to Live in Times like These" discuss complex and timely issues central to Christian faith.

The final two chapters are primarily of interest to mature, experienced Christians who find that advancing age brings a very different set of burdens altogether. In "How to Move Over" the emotional pitfalls as well as the practical aspects of coping with retirement are discussed in detail. "How to Dig Deeper" explores methods of growing in the Spirit for those who may already have experienced God's blessings for many years.

Making Life Count contains a wealth of information for all Christians. In addition, it is a valuable source book for teachers and for all people who desire to know God's will and to walk in Christ's footsteps. By focusing on spiritual and physical growth, Dr. Sumrall and his sons provide inspiration and instruction for daily Christian living.

The Editors

MAKING
LIFE
COUNT

1

How to Go Places

In striving to make life count, you must inevitably establish the basic priorities of life. To go through life without having thought through and determined your priorities, and then periodically measuring your life against those priorities, is like setting out to sail the ocean with no navigational instruments. You drift aimlessly, never knowing where you are or where you're going to land. To use another metaphor, if you aim at nothing particular in life, you're sure to hit it. The way to know you are accomplishing your goals is to establish and stick to those priorities that will lead to the desired ends.

The purpose of this chapter is to define and to provide examples of Christian values in terms of priorities and goal-setting, and also to discuss the application of those values in terms of competition and achievement. Let's first identify three basic priorities for every Christian.

Know God

The first and most important priority in life is to know God. We must know that God is our heavenly

Father, as the Lord's prayer declares: "Our Father in Heaven, hallowed be Your name" (Matt. 6:9). In order to know God as our Father, we must understand our relationship with Him. We must not think of God as a mean, vengeful, hateful destroyer of mankind. Our heavenly Father loves us dearly and allowed His only Son to die so that we might join His family.

If a person has a poor "father image," he is likely to have a poor image of God as his or her Father. In order to change that image, we must look into the Bible to see the true image of God as our loving heavenly Father who watches our every step and is willing to forgive our mistakes. Philip said to Jesus, "Lord, show us the Father, and it is sufficient for us." Jesus replied by saying, "Have I been with you so long, and yet you have not known Me?" (John 14:8–9). By this Jesus meant that to see Him was to see the Father.

The essential nature of God the Father is clearly shown in Jesus' parable of the prodigal son. The word *parable* is derived from a Greek word meaning "to throw alongside"; thus, a parable is a story "thrown alongside" certain truths in order to illustrate and explain them better. A parable is simply a convenient way to teach spiritual truths, and Jesus used parables frequently to communicate profound lessons in an easily understood manner.

The parable of the prodigal son was about a wealthy man and his two sons. The younger son was rebellious toward his father and wanted to get away from home and live the way he pleased. The Jewish law stated that a father was to give a double share of his possessions to his first son (see Deut. 21:17); thus, an older son inherited two-

thirds, and a younger inherited one-third. Occasionally a father would divide his property before
his death, but it was very unusual for a son to ask
his father to do so. In this story, the younger son
selfishly desired his share of the inheritance while
his father was still living. The father then divided
his property between his two sons.

The younger son ran away to a distant land, perhaps to a large city like Antioch or Rome. Eventually he spent all his money and was left without
food or shelter. Jesus did not tell us exactly what
the boy did with his inheritance, saying only, he
"wasted his possessions with prodigal living"
(Luke 15:13).

The boy probably had a wonderful time at first,
but after all his money was gone his new "friends"
also disappeared, and he was left alone. To make
matters worse, a famine spread over the country,
and many people went hungry, including the boy.
Finally he found work on a farm, feeding pigs. Remember that the Jews considered pigs to be un-
clean animals and would not even touch them,
much less eat them. Thus, in Jewish society, a person who tended swine had sunk as low as he could
go.

Coming to his senses, the younger son realized
how selfish and proud he had been, and how fool-
ishly he had lived. He regretted what he had done
to himself and to his father. He blamed no one else
for his deeds, but said, "I have sinned" (Luke
15:18). He decided to go home, to confess his sin,
and to ask for forgiveness. Since he had already
asked for and received his inheritance from his father, he planned to return as a hired hand on his
father's farm.

The father saw the boy coming while he was still far away and ran out to meet his wayward son. He welcomed him back before the boy even could finish his confession, and he called for his servants to bring clean robes to replace his son's rags. He gave his son a ring and a pair of shoes, indicating his full acceptance of the wandering child. A prize calf, to be used only on a special occasion, was killed to make a feast, and a joyous celebration began.

What about the older son, the sensible one who stayed home while his brother strayed? He was working in the fields when his brother returned, and as he approached the house he heard the sounds of celebration. When he learned that his brother had returned in disgrace but had been forgiven, the older brother was angry. He refused to join the celebration despite his father's pleas. The older son was harsh in his judgment of both his father and his younger brother, and he accused his father of being unfair. The story ends with no indication at all that the older brother ever changed his attitude and joined the celebration.

By examining the actions of the father in the parable, we can learn what Jesus was trying to teach us about our heavenly Father. The father in the parable treated both sons with tenderness and affection. Even though one son rebelled and went to a faraway land and the other son stayed home, their father loved them both equally and was always willing to forgive their faults. The two sons did not have to earn their father's love, for his love was not based on good behavior. He loved them because it was his nature as their father. Thus, we learn that God's love is free, not earned.

Also, the father's love did not cease after the younger son rebelled: even when the boy went away to live recklessly, the father still loved him. In the same way, God's love for us never changes—it is constant no matter what we do.

Recall that in the parable the father ran to meet his son. He put his love into action and demonstrated his care for his son by celebrating the boy's return. Similarly, God's love for us is active, not passive, and He celebrates our return to Him after we stray.

Finally, the father loved both of his sons the same, even though both were rebellious in different ways. Likewise, God's love for us is impartial. He loves the poorest just as much as the richest, the most rebellious as surely as the greatest saint.

The love of God for man is revealed by His Son's death on Calvary. The Word says, "Greater love has no one than this, than to lay down one's life for his friends" (John 15:13). We realize how much God loves us in relation to the price He paid when He allowed His only Son to stand in place of the world's sins.

Just think—the Trinity of Father, Son, and Holy Spirit was in harmony before time began, and the presence of Jesus on earth was the first time there was any separation in the communication, love, and togetherness of the divine Godhead. We will only begin to appreciate adequately what Jesus did in becoming man when we get to heaven.

The Old Testament demonstrated God's love in Jeremiah 31:3: "With lovingkindness I have drawn you." Notice He did not say "beat you," or "destroy and harm you"; by and through lovingkindness is God's way. The concept of a loving, heavenly Father is misrepresented when storms, floods, volcanoes, hailstones, lightning, and other disasters are called "acts of God." Nothing could be further from the truth because the Word reveals to us that God is love. God allows calamities because he allows man to have freedom of choice, as in the Garden of Eden, and sometimes man makes wrong decisions and has to suffer the consequences. Also, the whole creation bears the adverse effects of Adam's decision to sin in Eden (see Rom. 8:20–22).

Of course, the greatest verse in the Bible regarding God's love is John 3:16: "For God so loved the world that He gave His only begotten Son, that whoever believes in Him should not perish but have everlasting life." God's essence is love. He demonstrated His love when He sent the best heaven had to offer. God then gave His people the option of receiving or rejecting His gift. Rejecting God's gift takes the form of sin, and the penalty for sin is death, but the gift of God is eternal life

Examples of God's love are numerous. Look at the background of John Newton who wrote the inspiring hymn, "Amazing Grace." He was at one time a pirate who traveled the world in slave ships. Newton had run away from home at an early age and boarded a pirate ship as a stowaway. He was later discovered and was taught the evil tricks of the trade. He became a brawler, a whoremonger, and an altogether vile character.

At home, his prayerful mother believed her son would be a changed man one day and would be saved. But John Newton belittled and berated anyone who talked about God. He knew the right way but was opposed to it, and he continued living his pirate life and rebelling against God's authority.

Finally, John Newton was caught in an immense

storm while rounding Cape Hope in South Africa.
He cried out for mercy and gave his all to the Lord.
From that experience came the hymn "Amazing
Grace." Thus John Newton, like the prodigal son,
returned to a loving, heavenly Father who was
glad to receive him, and he left a memorial to
God's amazing love in music.

God's Peace

When any person comes into contact with almighty God, that person will encounter His peace.
Peace is the assurance that one's relationship with
God is positive. It does not mean the absence of
difficulty. Rather, it means that in the midst of difficulty, all is well. Today there are people who have
tried everything to gain peace in their souls, but
they will never find it until they find the Prince of
Peace.

Whenever angels encountered humans in the
Scripture, they brought messages of peace and
good will. The biblical concept of angels is often
neglected and frequently misunderstood, but regardless of what their appearances might mean,
angels have always been messengers of God's
peace.

In one case, an angel approached Gideon and
gave the Word of the Lord to him, calling him a
"mighty man of valor" (Judg. 6:12). The angel of
communication was Gabriel, whose appearance
always brought peace to those he visited. Daniel
received a message of peace from an angel, and the
shepherds watching their flocks the night of
Christ's birth were told, "Glory to God in the high-
est, and on earth peace, good will toward men!"
(Luke 2:14).

Mary the mother of Jesus was visited by an angel who saluted her and gave her a message from the Father. After Jesus had risen from the dead, the angels gave glad tidings to Mary Magdalene and the other Mary who had come to bring spices for Jesus' body.

The Bible tells us in Romans 5:1, "We have peace with God through our Lord Jesus Christ." When we know how much God loves us and shows us this peace, then we are candidates for the total plan God has for us.

Recently the topic of fear was discussed in a leading national magazine. The primary contributor toward fear was listed as "having no particular direction of life." This is where Christians should excel, since their direction comes from God.

God's Plan

God's plan in our lives is determined by two factors, the Word and the Spirit. The Word of God gives us God's direction through revelation. Solomon, who asked God for wisdom and was granted it more than any man who ever lived, said, "Trust in the LORD with all your heart, and lean not on your own understanding; in all your ways acknowledge Him, and He shall direct your paths" (Prov. 3:5–6).

John 16:13 indicates that the Holy Spirit will also direct us: "However when He, the Spirit of truth, has come, He will guide you into all truth; for He will not speak on His own authority, but what He hears He will speak; and He will tell you things to come."

Humankind has always sought direction in life. Those people who are washed in the blood of Jesus, who know their names are written in the

Lamb's Book of Life, have complete rest in the knowledge of God's sovereignty over their lives. They know that a good, kind, loving, heavenly Father will guide His children with the utmost care and concern for their well-being.

What Jesus told His desciples also applies to us: "It is your Father's good pleasure to give you the kingdom" (Luke 12:32). Your pleasure is in knowing God's will for your life. The Word of God is the will of God. If you follow the direction and purpose that God gives through His Word, which gives us clear guidance in the vast majority of decisions we need to make each day, and then place the application of the Word in your heart, God's Spirit will lead you along His perfect path.

Know Yourself

The second priority of life is to know yourself. You must know the strong points of your character and personality. Recognizing your assets, you can develop them to their fullest God-given potential. After knowledge of God, there is no more important knowledge than self-understanding, and there is no better investment than self-improvement. Knowing your abilities, how you relate to people, and so on also helps you to judge better how you can best serve Jesus and His church.

As vital as it is to know your strengths, it is equally crucial to know your weaknesses and limitations. No one person can do all things well. In certain areas, you will never develop great proficiency no matter how hard or long you work. The key again is to know yourself and to be happy with the way God made you, doing your utmost to develop your strengths and leaving other abilities to people more gifted in them.

Examine your life periodically, especially in the light of God's Word. Ask your friends and family members what strengths and weaknesses they see in you. Seek the leading of the Holy Spirit. Strive to know yourself, and then capitalize on those capabilities with which God has blessed you.

Know Your Neighbor

Our third priority is a directive from Jesus: "You shall love your neighbor as yourself" (Matt. 19:19). It is very important for us not to judge others, for judging is God's exclusive right. Instead, we must endeavor to understand and love the people who come into our spheres of influence. We must gain insight into the strengths, weaknesses, and attitudes of those who surround us. We can become sensitive to others by studying their likes, dislikes, and habits.

So we need to work at knowing, loving, and serving others. This must be a top priority of the believer's life. To love God is to love the people for whom His Son died.

Applying Priorities

Now that we have learned about three key priorities of life from a Christian perspective, let's apply them to our culture's predominantly competitive atmosphere. Many people are under the impression that Christians who "turn the other cheek" are unable to compete successfully with less scrupulous persons. In this section, we will show how and why Christians can, should, and do compete successfully without violating their Christian values.

In America, and in most other developed nations, competition is one of the cornerstones of society. At an early age people are taught to compete, to rise above the crowd, and to achieve the most possible in the shortest period of time. Competition provides the necessary motivation for many people, and when it is kept under control, it is a good thing. Competition is the basis for our free enterprise system in America. However, because of its importance, it is possible for the competitive drive to become a consuming passion that can threaten our very existence. Competition provides motivation, but it is essential for us to be motivated toward Christian goals with our priorities where they should be. Preoccupation with competition, not for the Lord's sake but for its own sake, distorts our perspective and causes us to have a self-centered attitude.

Most often competition becomes harmful to the individual who is overly concerned with the accumulation of material possessions. This is an example of wrongful goal-setting. With his life out of balance, such a person may find he has neglected to serve the Lord. Jesus pointed this out in Luke 21:34–35: "But take heed to yourselves, lest your hearts be weighed down with carousing, drunkenness, and cares of this life, and that Day come on you unexpectedly. For it will come as a snare on all those who dwell on the face of the whole earth."

At one time or another, most of us do become overly involved in worldly concerns and the accumulation of goods. At such times we fail to attend to family, prayer, Bible reading, and all the things that God would have us enjoy. Psalm 34:9 says, "Oh, fear the Lord, you His saints! There is no want to those who fear Him." There is nothing wrong with competition or with striving to get ahead, but we must never allow such ambitions to become our top priorities.

Some people rely on their own abilities to raise themselves above their peers. While not necessarily bad, this attitude can lead to using cutthroat methods to gain promotions and to handle stress and pressure. Such methods are unnecessary when God is in control. The psalmist wrote, "Blessed are the undefiled in the way, who walk in the law of the Lord!" (Ps. 119:1).

But you may ask, "How can I get ahead? What better way is there than promoting by myself?" The answer is simple: allow God to promote you rather than trying to promote yourself. This does not mean you should allow others to take advantage of you, but be wise as God gives you wisdom. James said in the first chapter of his epistle, "If any of you lacks wisdom, let him ask of God, who gives to all liberally and without reproach, and it will be given to him" (v.5). Psalm 73:24 says, "You will guide me with Your counsel,/And afterward receive me to glory." Letting God work through you to achieve His goals is the only way to succeed without developing future troubles. Paul wrote that God

will render to each one according to his deeds: eternal life to those who by patient continuance in doing good seek for glory, honor, and immortality; but to those who are self-seeking and do not obey the truth, but obey unrighteousness—indignation and wrath, tribulation and anguish" (Rom. 2:6–9).

Wisdom may require that you change the ways in which you compete. An executive once said about building his business: "Inch by inch, it's a cinch: yard by yard, it's hard." Making big changes all at once is hard for anyone, but small consistent changes will bring lasting results. It's like the story of the hare and the tortoise: the long-distance runner, not the sprinter, finally wins. Proverbs 4:18 says, "But the path of the just is like the shining sun,/That shines ever brighter unto the perfect day." If we work each day toward our goal of living in the light of the Lord and receiving His guidance, we will achieve lasting results, and our success is assured.

It is important to be motivated toward success, but it is more important to be motivated by Christian priorities and values and to seek Christian goals. Some people prefer to blame others rather than their own lack of effort for their failures. But God gives to each a measure of abilities and talents. In his first letter to Timothy, Paul said, "Do not neglect the gift that is in you" (1 Tim. 4:14).

In the parable of the talents told in Chapter 19 of Luke, each servant had the responsibility to make the most of what was given to him. The individual must decide whether to emulate the servant who invested a large portion for his master or the one who hid his money and produced no more.

Your motivation for succeeding must be correct in order for God to bless and help you. A desire to provide for your loved ones and to return to the Lord the tithe that belongs to Him is the correct attitude toward material gain, rather than the greedy desire to hoard wealth for its own sake. This may be difficult for many people to do, especially since there are many day-to-day pressures that encourage greedy behavior. However, giving to God is the most important part of success. And the best gift you can give Him is your love, expressed in a life controlled by His priorities.

2

How to Sit Tight

Timing is of the utmost importance in God's plan for you. The Bible says, there is a "time to tear, /And a time to sew; /A time to keep silence, / And a time to speak" (Eccles. 3:7). We all find ourselves in difficult circumstances occasionally. If we run away before our victory comes, we have missed our cue. This happens to all kinds of people, including pastors who have run out on their churches just before big victories, or business people who have quit and sold their businesses just before the hand of God reached out to them.

Whatever your battle, God will help you win it if you just sit tight. He can't do anything for you if you run away from the battle—what can He do for you if you are not there?

God is never in a hurry, but he is always on time. Our problem is that too often we do hurry, and as a result our timing is out of order. When a difficult situation demands action, determining the proper response is a dilemma many people never resolve. Knowing what to do when faced by adversity is what the concept of *sitting tight* is all about. Sitting tight is the answer to many of life's stormiest troubles and is one of life's greatest lessons.

What Is "Sitting Tight"?

What is sitting tight, and how is it done? Psalm 46:10 says, "Be still, and know that I am God." We ought to realize that when it seems disaster is about to strike is the time to rely on our faith in God and on the knowledge that He has a reason and a time for everything. We know that we are winners, not losers, because God wants us to live victoriously; so we must first seek His will. Sitting tight means seeking God's will for our lives and then waiting for Him to reveal His answers. Sitting tight works because it calls upon the power of God. Sitting tight requires self-appraisal, honesty, a sense of personal responsibility, and an uncommon amount of persistence. Sometimes God's will is hard to know, but it is our task to seek His will in all things.

It is very common for people to run away from their problems. It is so easy to run away! When young people run away from home, they are usually just running away from a few problems, not realizing that they will carry most of their troubles with them wherever they go. There are men who run away from their wives thinking it is the way to solve their marital problems. Problems, marital or otherwise, are not solved by retreating from them, but by confronting them head-on.

The United States leads the world in the number of people who change residences: about 15 percent of the total population moves each year. We move from house to house and from city to city until it seems that moving is one of our favorite pastimes. Why? It is as if we are trying to evade something. There is something desperately comical about such behavior, as indicated by the following humorous verse:

> I do not know, I do not care
> How far it is to anywhere;
> I only know that where I'm not
> Is always the alluring spot!

So much moving around speaks of a certain restlessness, a discontent with the way things are, and a desire to escape from one's troubles by running away from them. The Bible makes numerous references to people who faced hardship. There are tragic examples of individuals who refused responsibility and ran away from their problems, as well as more inspiring examples of others who faced their troubles squarely and emerged victorious. All of these biblical examples have one thing in common. Namely, they emphasize the importance of every person's decision about which of two paths to take: victory or failure. One thing is certain: it is easy to quit. Anybody can quit. Of course, quitters never win, just as surely as winners never quit. One must learn how to sit tight when there is a problem, for therein is the strength to overcome any hardship.

Sitting Tight under Adverse Circumstances

It has been said that a person's instinctive reactions under stress are the true test of his beliefs: thus, our greatest opportunities to sit tight and demonstrate our faith in God come when our lives are their stormiest. We all face different storms because we have our unique sets of circumstances to deal with. Loved ones may hurt us, our jobs may pressure us, or any number of other things may bring turbulence into our lives.

Storms in human events parallel storms in nature and are similar in a symbolic way of many common human problems. For example, we always try to take certain precautions against a storm before it occurs, and the time to prepare for an upcoming storm is when things are proceeding smoothly. When the storm finally breaks, we can then take shelter, and afterward we can enjoy the rainbow.

There are many kinds of storms. There are violent storms that rip through the countryside, leaving paths of destruction. There are mild storms that provide rain for growth or bring beautiful blankets of snow. Much can be learned by comparing the patterns of nature and the patterns of our lives.

Low pressure in the atmosphere is one cause of storms and the changes they bring. When our lives are stormy, often we feel "low" or depressed, and we are likely to create a "low pressure atmosphere" around ourselves. On the other hand, a high pressure system usually means fair weather: when things are going well for us, we usually feel good. When a low pressure system departs and fair weather is on the way, there is an accompanying cool breeze that refreshes and clears the air. We can have this refreshment also when storms come our way. When we receive the answers to our prayers and when the storms clear, we feel rejuvenated and ready for new tasks.

Another factor in the weather is the jet stream, which is a current of rapidly moving air flowing from east to west at an altitude of thirty to forty thousand feet. When the jet stream moves in a straight line, the weather moves in a regular pattern and there are few disruptions. If the jet stream veers sharply at an angle, instability and severe weather can result. In our own lives, when we make sharp turns or drastic changes, we may suffer instability and disruption. We should always make changes with care, seeking God to guide us in the right direction.

Biblical Storms

The first reference to a storm in the Bible is in Genesis, when God destroyed the earth with a flood because of rampant sin. Job called the wicked "chaff that a storm carries away" (Job 21:18). David said, "I would hasten my escape/ From the windy storm and tempest" (Ps. 55:8). In referring to his escape from those who would do him ill, David called his trouble a storm, a tempest. In Psalm 107, we see that God has control over storms: "He calms the storm,/So that its waves are still./ Then they are glad because they are quiet;/So he guides them to their desired haven" (vv. 29–30). God is our comforter in times of trouble, and he provides a haven of rest. He alone has the ability to banish the dark clouds from our horizon.

Biblical Examples of Sitting Tight

Let's look at several individuals in the Bible who knew the value of sitting tight during stormy periods in their lives. Elijah, the Shunammite woman, Sarah, Moses, Nehemiah, and Daniel are all excellent examples from the Old Testament of the various ways in which God may require a person to sit tight. Let's also study Jonah, who learned the wisdom of sitting tight the hard way, when he unsuccessfully tried to escape God's call.

Elijah

Elijah appears in the biblical narrative of God's judgment of a wayward and idolatrous Israel. Elijah performed his miracles during the life-or-death struggle between the worship of Yahweh and Baal worship. The adherence of the northern Israelites to the faith of their fathers was at issue, and all other questions regarding religious observances sank to minor importance. During this period, the tendency of Hebrew prophets to disagree with official state policy was a developing trend. Elijah was strongly opposed to the worship of pagan gods such as Baal and Asherah, a stance that often endangered his life by bringing him into con flict with those in power.

Elijah's prophetic activities demanded Israel's unconditional allegiance to Yahweh. The name *Elijah*, which means "the Lord is my God," may have been attributed to him because of his message and ministry, thus symbolizing what he said as well as who he was.

Elijah's prophetic zeal was particularly aimed at other official religious cults, and he was opposed to the accepted standards of the day, when belief in many gods was normal. In fact, to believe in only one god might have been interpreted as "unneighborly" and possibly hostile in the political and military context of the era.

Elijah's views especially conflicted with those of

King Ahab, Israel's monarch. Ahab had attempted to cultivate economic ties with Israel's neighbors, particularly Tyre. One of the consequences of such efforts was that the king had married Jezebel, a daughter of Ethbaal, king of the Sidonians. Ahab saw no harm in tolerating and participating in the religion of his neighbors, and in particular the religion of his wife. Therefore, he established a center of Baal worship at Samaria. After Ahab had given himself to the worship of Baal, Elijah made his first appearance.

With neither introduction nor prior reference to his lineage in the Bible, Elijah stepped into Israel's history. In 1 Kings 17, he declared to Ahab the onset of a drought. As punishment for building the temple for Baal at Samaria, Elijah predicted the drought would continue until he commanded otherwise.

According to James 5:17, Elijah himself prayed to the Lord for this drought. Probably he did so with the intention of showing Baal's impotence before the eyes of Israel. The Lord heard Elijah's request, and a terrible famine settled over the land. For the next three years, Elijah waited for a sign from God that it was time for the drought to end. Elijah probably had no idea at the time how matters would resolve themselves, but he was both patient and persistent in seeking God's will—a classic example of sitting tight.

Finally, when it seemed that Israel would perish from the drought, Elijah sought an audience with Ahab. Elijah challenged Ahab and the 450 prophets of Baal to a contest on Mount Carmel (see 1 Kings 18) in the presence of the people. Each side would offer sacrifices to its god without building a fire. The ignition of the fire was left to the deity, who would thereby reveal himself as the true God.

The prophets of Baal suffered a crushing failure despite their fervent prayers that their god send fire. Then Elijah gathered the people of Israel about an ancient altar of the Lord and repaired it using twelve stones, one each for the twelve tribes of Israel.

Elijah then dug a trench around the altar and ordered water to be poured on the sacrifice. Three times water was poured on the altar and the trench overflowed. Then Elijah prayed a simple prayer to God, asking Him to make himself known as the God of Israel.

> Then the fire of the LORD fell and consumed the burnt sacrifice, and the wood and the stones and the dust, and it licked up the water that was in the trench. Now when all the people saw it, they fell on their faces; and they said, "The LORD, He is God! The LORD, He is God!" (1 Kings 18:38–39)

Then Elijah commanded that the prophets of Baal be slaughtered, and rain was sent to end the drought.

According to 2 Kings 2:1–11, Elijah did not die but was carried bodily to heaven in a whirlwind, an honor previously bestowed only upon Enoch. Elisha, the only witness to this event, took up the mantle of Elijah that had fallen from him as he ascended and carried it as a token of his continuation of Elijah's ministry (see 2 Kings 2:13–14). Like Elijah and all the prophets who would follow him, Elisha emphasized the exclusivity of Israel's commitment to their God and the covenant responsibilities they had to each other.

This demonstration of God's power was the beginning of the restoration of Israel's faith in the one true God, and the lesson for us is clear: don't run away from your problems—sit tight and you can win. God made you a winner, and all you must do is have enough faith not to run away when times are hard.

The Shunammite Woman

There was a woman who showed great hospitality to the prophet Elisha. As a reward, she was blessed with a son because of Elisha's prayers on her behalf. Several years after the boy's birth, he died unexpectedly in his mother's arms. Instead of grieving, his mother decided the boy would live again, and she sought out Elisha's aid. When she found Elisha and he asked "Is all well?" she answered "All is well." She knew what she wanted, and by sitting tight and not fleeing she was able to get it. Elisha returned home with her, and indeed, he raised her son from the dead. The woman was not only faithful and patient, but she was also persistent. Thus, when all seems lost, sit tight. Belief in God and persistence in seeking His will, will enable you to claim His reward for you, not only in life but in eternity as well.

Sarah

One of the most interesting persons in the Bible is a woman named Sarah. Her story is an extreme example of faithful patience. When Sarah was a young woman, she was promised that through her husband Abraham she would become the mother of multitudes and kings. Yet as the years passed, she bore no children. God wanted her to wait for the proper time, and only God knows why Sarah had to wait for so many years. From the description given in the Bible, it is clear that Sarah's long wait was vital to God's plan.

What would you have done? Gone crazy? Screamed at everybody in the neighborhood? The Bible says that Sarah counted God faithful to what He had promised (see Hebrews 11:11). She was ninety-one years old when Isaac was born and Abraham was one hundred. God rewarded Sarah's patience, just as He rewards everyone who diligently and persistently seeks His will. Sarah was able to sit tight because she believed God's promise would be fulfilled.

Moses

Another example of the value of sitting tight comes from the story of Moses. He was raised in the Egyptian Pharaoh's palace, but as an adult he got into trouble and fled into the desert to save his life. Moses lived in the land of Midian for many years before God revealed Moses' purpose in His plan. Just think—Moses was a man who had been raised as a prince, but he had to tend sheep and just sit tight.

Finally God spoke to Moses from a burning bush about the task for which He had chosen him—to lead Israel out of slavery in Egypt. Perhaps God had been preparing the prince for forty long, grueling years in the desert as Israel's leader. Moses passed the test: he was content to sit tight for forty years to learn God's will, and he endured the dusty desert because he knew the value of sitting tight. Sitting tight enabled Moses to claim a mighty victory for Israel in God's name.

Nehemiah

We read in the Bible of a man named Nehemiah, who was the cupbearer to a pagan king. If ever a man was able to sit tight, he was the one. He asked the king of Persia, which ruled the land and people of Israel at the time, for permission to rebuild the walls of Jerusalem. His request was granted, but he had many enemies in the project. They mocked his efforts and threatened him. But Nehemiah sat tight, and eventually the city was rebuilt: the gates were installed and the palaces were restored, and all because one man knew how to sit tight in the face of discouraging opposition.

Daniel

Another inspiring example is Daniel, who served the Lord with all his heart. Daniel was a favorite of the heathen king Nebuchadnezzar of Babylon, who fed his prisoners from his own table. But Daniel refused to eat food that had been sacrificed to idols, so he entreated the king's chieftain to feed him and his friends a diet of vegetables and water for ten days. When Daniel and his companions were presented to the king, their physical and mental condition was far superior to that of the men who had eaten the king's delicacies. So Daniel was allowed to decline the king's food.

Later, Daniel had enemies who tried to kill him by urging the king to make a law they knew he would break, the punishment for which was imprisonment in a den of lions. But Daniel was not afraid, and he continued to pray to God three times a day despite the new ordinance against prayer. Daniel was eventually thrown into the den of lions as punishment, but he emerged unharmed.

God strengthened and protected Daniel because Daniel was secure in his faith, just as God will strengthen and protect you if you put your trust in Him and sit tight.

Jonah

There are also examples in the Bible of people who did not sit tight. The most prominent of these is an evangelist and prophet named Jonah. When God called him to go to Nineveh to preach, Jonah balked and fled in the opposite direction instead. Jonah set out to cross the Mediterranean in a ship, "but the Lord sent out a great wind on the sea,...so that the ship was about to be broken up" (Jon. 1:4). God sent the storm to halt Jonah's flight. The ship's cargo was lost, and finally the sailors cast lots and determined that Jonah was the cause of their ill fortune. They tried to row to safety, but finally they heeded Jonah's advice and threw him overboard. The seas were calmed and Jonah was swallowed by a large fish that coughed him onto dry land three days later. Only then did Jonah obey the Lord and travel to Nineveh.

If Jonah had sat tight, he wouldn't have had to go through all that misery. Subsequently, Jonah was able to save not only himself but also the entire city of Nineveh after he decided to obey God.

After Jonah preached in Nineveh, he was still unable to sit tight. He moaned and complained because the people repented! Imagine an evangelist's going to a city to have a revival and getting angry when his ministry is effective! That is a kind of person Jonah was—he could not sit tight and win great victories. He could have gone down in history as a much greater person if he had been able to trust God more.

In our lives there are moments of decision like the one Jonah faced. In turning from God's will, Jonah brought only strife to himself and those around him. Our lives will be similarly stressful unless we accept God's call, whether it is to go to Nineveh, find a new job, enter the ministry, or do whatever else God may require of us. Is the Lord telling you to do something you are running from?

If you have a problem in your home, trust God and sit tight. If your job causes you stress, sit tight. Sitting tight has never lost a battle, whereas fleeing and quitting as Jonah did has lost many. You don't have to take extreme measures every time something happens that doesn't please you— just sit tight, and God will provide an answer for those who trust in Him.

Jesus was in the midst of many storms during His ministry. In the temple, in the crowds, and while working with people, He was often the center of controversy. Jesus undoubtedly knew how to sit tight, as His behavior in the days and hours leading Him to Calvary attest. However, the disciples occasionally had difficulty understanding how Jesus could be so calm during a crisis. Jesus' instructions to them at such times are straightforward lessons in sitting tight.

On the Sea of Galilee

One of the greatest examples of sitting tight is the account of Jesus and the disciples on the Sea of Galilee. A furious storm rose and tossed their boat about, but Jesus, far from being concerned about their danger, was asleep! The disciples awoke Him, afraid they would die in the storm. Jesus said to them, "'Why are you fearful, O you of little faith?' Then He arose and rebuked the winds and the sea. And there was a great calm" (Matt. 8:26). Jesus had the authority and the right to rebuke the storm. When we are born again, we, too, have the power and the authority to calm the storms that arise in our lives. God wants you to be steady, and through the power of Jesus you can calm any storm, no matter how violently it rages or how threatening it seems.

You Can Do It

As you read this, you may be about to run away from your job, your family, or your self. "I can't endure it any more!" you say. Yes, with God's help, you can. It is wrong to run away—be a winner right where you are. You can do it by trusting God's plan for you and by sitting tight.

At this point, let us consider one qualification to the principle of sitting tight. If you are in physical danger, you should certainly act with prudence to remove yourself from that danger; you should not submit to physical attack. No one has the right to abuse another person. In cases of physical abuse, temporary escape until conditions improve may be necessary.

God's Word tells us, "Fear not, for I am with you; be not dismayed, for I am your God. I will strengthen you, yes, I will help you, I will uphold you with my righteous right hand" (Isa. 41:10). God is our strength and our comfort regardless of our circumstances. If God is for us, who can stand against us?

We must learn to sit tight in moments of crisis, for it is the moment of decision under pressure that causes us to panic. When we panic, we fail to seek God's will and forget to rely on His peace. By sitting tight, seeking God's plan for our lives, and remaining calm, we will find that God's peace is far more satisfying than anything we could do alone. As the apostle Paul told us, "Be anxious for nothing, but in everything by prayer and supplication, with thanksgiving, let your requests be made known to God; and the peace of God, which surpasses all understanding, will guard your hearts and minds through Christ Jesus" (Phil. 4:6–7).

3

How to Look Up

At one time or another each of us is discouraged, disheartened, downtrodden, and downcast. For some people this is a temporary condition, but for others it is a seemingly perpetual state of affairs. It is vitally important for Christians to know how to overcome such dark times. The Christian who cannot look up cannot be an effective witness for Christ and cannot praise God. Will the world be attracted to Christ if Christians are depressed and dissatisfied? Of course not. Therefore, in this chapter we will focus on four suggestions for surviving times of depression: *know and trust God, possess a strong spirit, make the right choices, and deal with crisis.*

Know and Trust God

Have you ever thought about David's being a discouraged man? He was, but he didn't stay that way. He had the ability to bounce back from every bad situation. He had the ability to encourage himself, to stop a downward trend and go in the right direction. "Why are you cast down, O my soul?" (Ps. 43:5) was a very important for David to ask. He showed the ability to analyze himself and deal with his feelings.

David may have learned an important lesson as a boy while tending his father's sheep. The only company he had for many years in the Judean hills were the sheep, the sun, the stars, the moon, and God. In the wilderness, a flock of any size was subject to attack by predators such as bears or lions. Since he was alone, he had no defense other than his own physical strength and the strength that came from God.

In telling King Saul of his experiences as a shepherd, David said that when bears and lions came to take his sheep, he would go after them and kill them. David understood that it was not because of his own physical strength that he was able to slay wild beasts, but that it was through God's intervention (see 1 Sam. 17:34–37). He also understood the love and compassion of God.

Yet David's life was not easy, as he experienced much betrayal and many attempts on his life over the years. Some of his worst moments were of his own doing, however. Perhaps the most well known of these was his adultery with Bathsheba and his subsequent murder of her husband, Uriah.

This familiar story is told in 2 Samuel, and we see God's judgment come upon David for his sins in chapter 12. There, God's prophet Nathan came to David the king and confronted him with the facts of his transgressions. Nathan told David that the punishment for what he had done was to be the death of the child who had been born out of David's adultery.

Even though David's motives and actions had been wrong, he nevertheless loved Bathsheba and the child she had given him; so Nathan's prophecy threw David into a great depression. The Bible tells us that when the child became sick, David refused to eat and spent all night lying on the ground, begging God to spare the child's life. Those of us who are parents can appreciate the misery David must have experienced.

This state of affairs continued for seven days, and then the child died. It would have been easy for David to go into an even deeper depression from which he might never have recovered.

That is exactly what David's servants expected him to do:

> And the servants of David were afraid to tell him that the child was dead. For they said, "Indeed, while the child was still alive, we spoke to him, and he would not heed our voice. How can we tell him that the child is dead? He may do some harm!" (2 Sam. 12:18)

However, when David learned the child was dead, he surprised his servants by doing the opposite of what they had anticipated. "So David arose from the ground, washed and anointed himself, and changed his clothes; and he went into the house of the LORD and worshiped. Then he went to his own house; and when he requested, they set food before him, and he ate" (2 Sam. 12:20).

In other words, David recovered immediately from his depression and went on about the business of living. But how could he overcome his grief so quickly? The answer is found in Psalm 51, which David wrote after these experiences. He said to the Lord, "For I acknowledge my transgressions,/And my sin is before me./Against You, You only, have I sinned,/And done this evil in Your sight/....Create in me a clean heart, O God,/And renew a steadfast spirit within me" (Ps. 51:3–4, 10). David showed his great understanding of God and his recognition of his own sinfulness, and he sought God's mercy.

David went on to say, "For You do not desire sacrifice, or else I would give it;/You do not delight in burnt offering./The sacrifices of God are a broken spirit,/A broken and a contrite heart—/These, O God, You will not despise" (Ps. 51:16–17). David acknowledged that he had not been seeking to please God, that far from being broken and contrite, his heart had grown arrogant toward God and His law. He had disregarded everything he knew to be right in pursuing his relationship with Bathsheba and having her husband killed.

Here, then, is the lesson for us: David saw in the terrible circumstance of his son's death a reminder of who God is and what He expects of His people, and David knew that after his confession, the mercy and forgiveness of God would be his. Reassured of those facts, he could put his sorrow behind him and go on with his life. The key is that David knew God intimately, and he came out of the situation with a renewed resolve to follow the Lord. His focus had shifted from his sinful desires to the great God of heaven.

Now let's apply David's experience to our times of depression. At various times in our lives, we are all faced with difficult circumstances—at work, at home, at school—that can lead very easily to depression. And as we slide into depression, we tend to lose sight of everything but ourselves and our worries. At such times we, like David, need to be reminded that God is loving, sovereign, and merciful. We need to get our attention off ourselves and back on the Lord. As He has proved faithful and all-sufficient in the lives of biblical people like David, and as he has proved Himself in our own lives in the past, so the Lord can help in the present distress if we turn to Him and trust Him. Knowing that, we can move forward in life and meet its challenges victoriously rather than allow them to plunge us into depression.

Possess a Strong Spirit

It is a popular misconception that Christians should be weak and spineless, with no backbone. This is not the case at all. In God's Word there are numerous examples of people of God who were strong in spirit. Moses was one; he fought against the Pharaoh and his army. At the Red Sea, he showed confidence in God's Word when he directed the Israelites to be still and see the Lord's salvation. The Pharaoh's army was about to drive them into the water, but he knew the Lord would fight for them.

David also faced tremendous adversity and emerged victorious because of his strong spirit. Even as a young man, David demonstrated God's faithfulness in his match against Goliath. Declaring to the defiant Philistine that the Lord would deliver him into his hands, David declared the battle to be the Lord's and showed that the Lord saves.

Speaking to the children of Israel in 2 Chronicles 32:7–8, Hezekiah said, "Be strong and courageous; do not be afraid nor dismayed....With Him is an arm of flesh; but with us is the LORD our God, to help us and to fight our battles." God will remain the same tomorrow as He is today, and we can rejoice knowing that He will help us fight our battles both today and tomorrow.

The development of a strong spirit is more a preventative than a cure for the depths of depression. In other words, a strong spirit develops over a period of time and as a result of long communion with God. It is not something you can generate instantly when trials come. If you do not already have a strong spirit, it will not be available to aid you during those times.

However, a strong spirit, a spirit of boldness and faith in God, should be the goal of every Christian anyway. We should be striving constantly to grow in the Lord and to develop that strength God has given each of us. The Bible tells us, "God has not given us a spirit of fear, but of power and of love and of a sound mind" (2 Tim. 1:7).

This strength of spirit grows out of the knowledge of and trust in the Lord we discussed in the previous section. If you know and trust God, you have the power to face difficult situations because you know He will give what you need when you need it.

Be careful, however, not to confuse godly strength of spirit with arrogance or self-confidence. Godly strength comes from the Lord and is developed out of a relationship with Him. The human heart is deceptive and proud, and it is easy to slip into the sin of taking the credit for something He has done and for which He alone deserves the glory. Jeremiah 17:9 tells us, "The heart is deceitful above all things, and desperately wicked." So do not make the mistake of thinking you will ever grow strong to the point of not needing the Lord any more. When oppression comes, and with it depression, it is the strength of God that will be sufficient for your needs.

When you have grown strong in the Lord, you will be able to face oppression with the faith of a Job: "Though He slay me, yet will I trust Him" (13:15). That is strength enough to overcome depression! You will be able to say with the psalmist, "God is our refuge and strength,/A very present help in trouble./Therefore we will not fear" (Ps. 46:1–2).

Make the Right Choices

How do you come through? Do you come through difficult situations with your head bent, with your heart bruised, or do you come through with your spirit refreshed and ready for new challenges? It is up to each of us to determine whether we will allow difficult problems or circumstances to overwhelm us or whether we will prevail and emerge with renewed vigor.

We are all faced with choices every day. These begin with the most mundane things—"do I wear red or blue today?" "Do I eat cereal or eggs for breakfast?" From there, of course, the importance and consequences of our choices escalate up to the most crucial issues of life. Different people have different abilities in decision making, but under normal circumstances most of us function reasonably well in this area.

When we become depressed, however, our ability to make decisions is greatly impaired. Thinking is not as clear as usual. Wisdom is clouded. The

will to persevere and overcome is sapped by a feeling of helplessness and hopelessness. All of these
make it more difficult to reach good decisions, or
any decision at all in some cases.

Yet those times when we are depressed are also
times we can least afford to make poor decisions
because such decisions can have devastating consequences, and the negative effects can last a long
time and be very difficult to overcome.

An excellent illustration of a poor decision made
in the depths of depression is in 1 Samuel 28. The
prophet Samuel had just died, and King Saul was
about to go into battle against the Philistines.
"When Saul saw the army of the Philistines, he
was afraid, and his heart trembled greatly" (v. 5).
Saul was fearful and depressed in the face of the
enemy, and he needed guidance. Because of his
disobedient heart, however, God refused to give
Him any message. Feeling deserted by the Lord,
Saul must have grown even more depressed—to
the point of desperation.

What did he do then? He decided to take an
action expressly forbidden by God. He chose to
consult a medium he thought could conjure up
Samuel's spirit from the dead so he could ask him
what to do. Saul himself had only recently ordered
all mediums and spiritists out of Israel, knowing
they were contrary to God's law (see 28:3; also Lev.
20:27).

To the medium's shock, Samuel did appear, and
his news for Saul was all bad. He said, "Why then
do you ask me, seeing the Lord has departed from
you and has become your enemy?...Moreover the
Lord will also deliver Israel with you into the hand
of the Philistines. And tomorrow you and your

sons will be with me" (28:16, 19).

The result, as we might expect, was that Saul was devastated. "Then immediately Saul fell full length on the ground, and was dreadfully afraid because of the words of Samuel" (28:20). And the next day, true to Samuel's prophecy, Saul and his sons were killed by the Philistines, and the entire Israelite army was crushed.

It is vital that we understand *before* depression comes how important our decisions in such times will be, and how much more we will need the grace of God's guidance. Therefore, develop the habit now of seeking the Lord's leading in the decisions you make. Always include your requests as part of your routine. Then, when trials come, the habit of seeking the Lord's guidance rather than turning inward will help you make better decisions and in turn you can overcome your depression faster and more completely.

The advice of godly friends can also be tremendously helpful when you know your own decision-making ability is not up to par. Seek out those friends and listen to the wisdom the Lord has taught them through their experiences. Combined with your prayers and the counsel of God's Word, their advice can help you make good decisions and avoid the kind of disaster that befell Saul.

Deal with Crisis

Many times I have observed people in airline terminals or on the street, and I have noticed very often that they seem to be unhappy. Their shoulders are bent, their expressions scowl, and they seem either angry or disdainful toward the human race.

There are many reasons why people may be in such a condition, but one thing is universally true: life without Christ is not worth living! This is especially true when we are confronted by responsibilities and pressures from our work, our family, our peers, and our awareness of national and international current events. Criticism, sin, and sorrow—and the depression they bring—can bend us all to the breaking point. In a real sense, they present us with crises.

The first step to rising above a crisis is to acknowledge that you are in one. It is surprisingly easy to be unaware of exactly what is happening to you and how you are modifying your behavior because of your problems. People can be so blind to trouble that their problems become insurmountable before they realize what is happening. Sin often impairs their ability to recognize problems.

King David saw the condition of his soul and knew he needed forgiveness. He said in Psalm 25:11–18,

> For Your name's sake, O LORD
> Pardon my iniquity, for it is great.
> Who is the man that fears the LORD?
> Him shall He teach in the way He chooses.
> He himself shall dwell in prosperity,
> And his descendants shall inherit the earth.
> The secret of the LORD is with those who fear Him,
> And He will show them His convenant.
> My eyes are ever toward the LORD,
> For He shall pluck my feet out of the net.
> Turn yourself to me, and have mercy on me,
> For I am desolate and afflicted.
> The troubles of my heart have enlarged;
> Oh, bring me out of my distresses!

Look on my affliction and my pain,
And forgive all my sins.

Forgiveness is waiting for those who will receive it; just ask.

The second step in dealing with crisis is to learn to correct a mistake as soon as you make it. The embarrassment involved in admitting a mistake causes many people to refuse even to acknowledge their errors. But if some attitude or action on your part is responsible for the crisis in which you find yourself, you must admit it and immediately move to rectify the situation. The longer you let something go without correcting it, the more difficult and expensive (emotionally, spiritually, financially) it will be to straighten matters out when you finally decide to act.

Third, you must be willing to accept help. The Lord is your help and salvation; you must be willing to accept the help He provides and to accept His plan for your life. God has given you certain natural abilities, and you must cooperate with Him to make the most of these talents. It is foolish to try to do what God has not called you to do. Success is achieved by working within your own abilities and by living uprightly before God.

Fourth, praise God ceaselessly. The positive attitude that comes from praising God can be tremendously uplifting. Praise can lift your spirits higher than anything you could do on your own. Look for Scriptures that speak of praise—there are more than four hundred of them. For example, Genesis 14:20 says "Blessed be God Most High who has delivered your enemies into your hand." The psalms are filled with "praise passages." An interesting and profitable exercise would be to read the psalms to locate all the passages praising God and then to keep the list of them for reference.

Praising and tithing can bring God's rewards into your life. All you must do is receive from the Lord the good things He has in store for you. Hold yourself up straight, and "let the heavens rejoice, and let the earth be glad; and let them say among the nations, 'The Lord reigns' " (1 Chron. 16:31).

When we must put ourselves in God's care in order to overcome depressing circumstances, we learn that He equips His children with the spiritual armor necessary to triumph over gigantic obstacles. Possessing a strong spirit enables us to admit mistakes and seek God's will for our lives. Making the right choices with God's help provides the renewal and rejuvenation everyone needs in order to continue to seek new challenges, and acknowledging and dealing with crisis enable us to praise God and receive His blessings.

4

How to Achieve Your Potential

Just as in nature tadpoles become frogs and caterpillars become butterflies, so also does a human being's growth follow a progressive path. Immaturity is replaced with maturity, and irresponsibility gives way to responsibility. Only humans have the ability to reflect on past experiences. This ability to learn and grow from past situations carries with it an implicit responsibility to do so, for otherwise humans are no better than animals. The person who is willing to examine his own life can discover untapped resources within himself that will help him realize his individual potential.

Understand Yourself

The first step toward self-awareness is the willingness to look within. The second step, surprisingly, is not to look too long! Attempting to make objective assessments about yourself is beneficial, but not to the extent that it paralyzes you through self-consciousness.

The purpose of self-examination is twofold. First, it serves to make you aware of your personal strengths and weaknesses. Second, it enables you to discover areas that prevent you from reaching your potential, where improvements are needed. The greater the insight you possess about your essential nature and your motives, the more you can be in control of your actions and your destiny. Perfect self-knowledge, though never really attained, is your goal. However, you can and should commit yourself to the lifelong battle to come to a greater understanding of your strengths and weaknesses.

In appraising and understanding your past, you are faced with two alternatives. You can use the past as an excuse for your present condition and for remaining as you are, or you can learn from your past in an effort to reach your peak. Sooner or later, everyone attempts self-improvement. Those who are successful begin with the realization that they cannot blame external circumstances, past or present, for who they are.

Fantastic results can occur when a person examines his past objectively and is able to learn from it. It is possible to learn not only from past tragedies but also from past joys. Pleasant past experiences form the basis for hope and for future happiness. The fact that hope for the future is an essential ingredient in self-improvement was expressed in Proverbs: "Where there is no vision, the people perish" (Prov. 29:18 KJV).

It is important to plan for your success and growth, for otherwise you will limit your success. A helpful technique for planning to succeed is projection. *Projection* means imagining you are succeeding in your quest to accomplish a goal. Many top-level business executives report that, prior to important meetings, they project images of themselves in their own minds and imagine what the best possible results of the meetings could be. The most successful athletes also mention being able to visualize running faster, jumping farther, making the big catch, or scoring the winning point as an important factor in their successes.

Projection enables you to react to your best advantage when you must make decisions rapidly, and it provides you with a game plan for handling difficult or stressful situations. The less you examine the path you have chosen, the thornier it will become. Your chances of victimizing yourself are much greater if you are not fully aware of what you are doing or why you are doing it.

What does the Bible say about self-knowledge? How should the Christian think of himself? On one hand is the teaching that, like Adam, all have sinned and rebelled against God's authority. On the other hand, all men are created in God's image. This duality within each of us is one of the central truths of our existence. The full revelation of the gospel puts matters into perspective: "You shall know the truth, and the truth shall make you free" (John 8:32). Because Jesus has taken away our sins, "if we confess our sins, He is faithful and just to forgive us our sins and to cleanse us from all unrighteousness" (1 John 1:9). Christians should not allow sin to blind them to the reality of God's forgiveness. His forgiveness is essential to a healthy self-concept, which in turn is necessary for personal Christian growth leading to the fulfillment of potential. God has created each of us with the potential for a worthy self-concept.

The greatest commandment is to love God. The second commandment is to love others as we love ourselves. Love of self is necessary for loving other people, and a positive self-image is our way of confirming that we have accepted God's blessings.

Self-love is tied to self-understanding. Because some people have difficulty loving themselves, they invent substitutes for self-worth. These substitutes may take many forms, but all of them are *defense mechanisms* that actually conceal low self-esteems. One such defense mechanism is involvement in an overly large number of activities. The person who does this is saying, "Look at how much I do: I must be an important person." Another substitute for self-worth is self-exaggeration. We have all met people who try to "sell" themselves to other people by boasting about their great deeds. Such people are often quite sensitive to criticism since they really have grave doubts about their own adequacy. Similarly, self-contempt is a common substitute for self-worth. Those who practice self-contempt try to mask their inadequacies by finding reasons for self-hate.

Note that self-love and selfishness are not the same thing; in fact, they are opposites. He who lacks a sense of self-worth may be preoccupied with himself and as a result is unable to reach out to others. In contrast, the person who has a strong love for himself has the capacity to love others and to care about their concerns as well as his own.

In order to know yourself, you must be willing to accept what your past teaches you about yourself. You must examine your hopes for the future to learn how they influence the present, and you must arrive at a view of yourself that enables you to appraise yourself objectively. When you have done this, you are ready to go on toward achieving your God-given potential.

Forming Goals

Self-knowledge is essential to achieving your potential, for without it, you will be unable to form effective goals. When forming goals it is important to be aware of the criteria you use in the process. So here we want to consider some suggestions for appropriate goal-setting. Goals should be liberating, person-oriented, relative to potential, specific, and flexible.

Goals can give meaning and purpose to life, but only if they are liberating. When a goal loses its attractiveness and its desirability, it ceases to be a goal and becomes a duty. Of course, duty can serve many useful purposes, but when it is unpleasant duty, it is harder to pursue. Thus, if Christians base their lives in Christ primarily on duty and obligation, they miss the vitality and spontaneity available to them. Our life in Christ is meant to be joyful, and we should take joy in the accomplishment of our Christian goals. The person who feels only a sense of duty is inclined to be less effective and less productive than a person who takes joy in his work, and goals should be chosen accordingly.

There is also a significant difference between task-oriented and person-oriented goals. Task-oriented goals, although often necessary or worthwhile for their own sakes, may not necessarily be growth goals. For example, everyone must earn a certain amount of money in order to survive. But a person who devotes his entire attention to the accumulation of wealth does nothing for his own personal growth and in fact may be limiting his growth. No matter how much money such a person accumulates, happiness and fulfillment are no closer to him than they were before his success. By contrast, person-oriented tasks seek the well-being of the individual through establishing and strengthening relationships. The primary reason for all activities of this sort is the growth of the person.

It is further necessary to set goals that reflect our potential. Because of the nature of goals, it is common to speak of them as "long-term" or "distant," expressions that denote lofty aspirations. However, envisioning such lofty possibiities can be a terrifying experience. Many people fear their potential for greatness, probably because it contains the potential for failure. Many people choose not to attempt to realize their potential in order to avoid that possibility of defeat.

It is true that failure to achieve unrealistic goals is depressing, but the fault in such cases is with the goal, not the person. It is necessary to take risks in order to make gains—the true difficulty is in determining whether certain goals are realistic or out of reach. In making this determination, two factors are primary. First, examine your depth of commitment to the goal. This will directly affect the amount of time and energy you expend in achieving it. Second, consider how long it will take to realize the goal. Some goals require a lifetime, while others may never be realized. It is important to give yourself enough time to accomplish your chosen goal.

Once you have set a specific and realistic goal,

you very likely will reach it. A good test to see if your goals are specific is to ask yourself if your goals are clear enough to be written down. If you cannot express your goals in writing, you probably need to think more about *exactly* what your goals are.

Although goals should be as precise as possible, it is advisable not to take them too literally. There is always the unforeseen possibility that something can alter plans and demand reassessments. We cannot know exactly what God plans to do tomorrow. As the book of James says, "Come now you who say, 'Today or tomorrow we will go to such and such a city, spend a year there, buy and sell, and make a profit'; whereas you do not know what will happen tomorrow....Instead you ought to say, 'If the Lord wills, we shall live and do this or that'" (4:13–15).

Also, since Christian growth is a never-ending process, the goals we set should never indicate that we plan to reach a certain plateau and then stop. The Holy Spirit knows no limit. Openness to new experiences, new revelations, and new goals is consistent with New Testament teaching.

Finally, goals should be shared with those close to you. Your friends and family can provide much encouragement and support as you strive to reach your potential. Your goals are like a road map, which you can consult when you come to a crossroads. The support of loved ones can provide motivation in the right direction.

Seeking Guidance

One very important consideration arises concerning what each of us wants from life. As mentioned earlier, hope for the future is a vital aspect of self-understanding, for without it we are doomed to repeat unhappy past experiences. It is relatively easy to take the advice of teachers and guidance counselors while you are young and in school, but ultimately each of us must make an individual choice about which direction to take and which goals to pursue. Proverbs 22:6 (AMP) tells us, "Train up a child in the way he should go (and in keeping with his individual gift or bent) And when he is old he will not depart from it."

There are undoubtedly numerous people who dislike their chosen occupations, yet who remain in them because of monetary concerns. Such persons have what might be called a *false sense of obligation.* They imagine that they have no choice but to continue in the work that makes them miserable, and as a consequence they become maladjusted and unhappy. God does not intend for life to be this way. We can find fulfillment and peace if we strive to realize the potential that God has given us. Our task is to discover and to use the gifts and talents He has already provided, and in this we must seek His guidance.

In seeking guidance, many people turn to their friends and families, job counselors, or their pastors. Another excellent source of information is the many good books that have been written to help people analyze their interests and abilities and then see how these can be translated into jobs that would be fulfilling. It is important to remember, however, that consulting other people or books is only a starting point. Ultimately no one can make appropriate or even adequate decisions about your life and your self-concept besides you yourself.

The ultimate source of help and guidance comes from God, who is always there when we need Him and who is the only one truly able to judge us. God has planned for you to reach your potential, and He will instruct you if you are willing to listen to His Word.

Maintain Integrity

Being a person of integrity is another vital quality for attaining your potential. *Integrity* comes from the Latin word *integer* which means "whole." Thus, your loyalty cannot be divided if you possess integrity since firm adherence to values and principles is what integrity means. For Christians, integrity means becoming one with God, for only when we find Him are we truly whole. Integrity also means that our word is reliable: Jesus said, "let your 'yes' be 'yes,' and your 'no,' 'no' " (Matt. 5:37). In other words, we should mean what we say and say what we mean. Reliability is central to a person's character, especially for Christians. When a Christian commits himself to a certain course of action or undertakes any responsibility, the successful completion of the task brings honor to and approval from the heavenly Father.

Recall the story of Alexander the Great who felt lenient toward the state's prisoners and decided to release them all on a certain day. He spoke with a young man who was imprisoned and asked the prisoner if the charges brought before him were correct. The prisoner affirmed that the charges were true, and Alexander asked the prisoner, "What is your name?"

The young soldier replied, "Alexander, sir."

Startled, the king again screamed, "What is your name?"

To that the prisoner replied again, "Alexander, sir."

At this point the king picked up the prisoner and threw him to the ground, saying, "Either change your name or change your ways."

Just as Alexander the Great wanted his name to represent certain qualities, so also should we strive to be known as persons of integrity, for by doing so we praise God and glorify ourselves as well. Integrity is God-given, and by and through the Word of God it is developed. Psalm 119:89 says, "Forever, O LORD,/Your word is settled in heaven." We are God's children by virtue of the relationship brought about by the blood of Jesus Christ, and therefore we should strive for godly attitudes, desires, and actions. Reliability is essential to accomplishing this goal. This quality could be helpful in our factories, our businesses, and in our institutions of higher learning.

Guard against Apathy

A great part of our society today is apathetic to such concerns, and often this dangerous attitude is contagious. Reliable people—people who achieve their potential—are concerned about the quality of their work, about being fair both to employers and to employees, and about the human race; consequently, apathy and reliability are incompatible.

Apathy can be overcome by making goals and having dreams, for these are what motivate us to greater accomplishments. Faithfulness and obedience are the key ingredients for achieving your dream. The pivotal point is your inner desires, which ultimately determine who you are and what you do.

We may compare the development of our spiritual lives with the construction of a building. When looking at a building, we do not see the foundations of it. All we see are the outside walls, the embellishments, the facade. Yet the most important part of the building is its underlying structure, which prevents its collapse and provides a strong, solid edifice. God is in our lives using "building materials" to erect for Himself a holy habitation. Just as the building's foundation is planned by an engineer who knows how much stress to provide for, so also are the foundations of our lives planned by God, who provides for all our needs. And just as a building must be able to stand erect during strong winds, so must we be flexible to adapt to new situations when the winds of adversity blow. Let us be like the bamboo and not the oak, for the bamboo bends during the typhoon while other trees are snapped in two.

Dare to Dream

There are many examples in the Bible of people who achieved their potential through positive thinking, goal-setting, and dreaming. A prominent example of how dreams can become reality is the story of Joseph. Often when we speak of dreams we are referring to hopes and ambitions, and indeed these can become reality through God's Word. However, Joseph's sleeping dreams were to become reality.

God spoke to Joseph in a dream, which he related to his parents and brothers. He amazed them by saying that they would bow to him even though he was the youngest. This caused his brothers to despise him: and when their father showed his preference for Joseph by giving him a coat of many colors, they could take no more and resolved to kill him. They finally sold him into slavery, after which Joseph was taken to Egypt. In Egypt, Joseph's ability to understand and interpret dreams enabled him to rise in position and in prestige until he was second only to the Pharaoh in power. Joseph's understanding of dreams was the key to his future, and by remaining faithful to God, Joseph was able to achieve his potential for greatness.

Similiarly, Moses dared to dream. His dream was that one day Israel would be free from slavery and would become a great nation. God inspired this dream in Moses and used him to make the dream a reality. God had plans for the nation of Israel that were tied to Moses' dream, and by achieving his own personal potential as a leader, Moses helped Israel realize her potential as a nation.

To achieve your potential, keep in mind the advice of Matthew 6:33: "But seek first the kingdom of God and His righteousness, and all these things shall be added to you."

5

How to Stand Tall

Proverbs 10:9 underlines how important it is for Christians to stand tall, both before God and before humanity: "He who walks with integrity walks securely, but he who perverts his ways will become known." Personal situation and position in the world notwithstanding, every Christian's place in the body of Christ depends on his or her integrity. It is of the utmost importance to know how to walk uprightly in order to find God's plan for your success. Competition will be easier and success will be surer if you follow the principles set out in God's Word and abide by them.

Luke 2:52 says "And Jesus increased in wisdom and stature, and in favor with God and men." We know that Jesus is our best example of how to live and that we should emulate Him. How can we do as He did? How can we grow, both as Christians and as individuals? How can we stand tall in a world that tries to bend us, burden us, and weaken our step?

It is beautiful and amazing that, even though Jesus was the Son of God, He increased in stature. The clear lesson here is that we always have room for improvement and that to stand tall we must be able to grow. To maintain an upright spiritual posture, we must continually seek God's will for our lives, which means we are always growing closer to Him.

How Tall Are You?

One of the most important lessons in learning to stand tall is to realize that *you are important.* Regardless of what you think of yourself right now, you are an important and vital part of God's plan. You can be as important as you want to be, simply by wanting to and by following His will. Understanding that you are important enables you to stand tall. Take pride in yourself so that God can be proud of you as well. You were created in God's image; thus, it is difficult to glorify God and to berate yourself at the same time.

Another fundamental lesson in standing tall is understanding that *you were born for victory,* not for defeat. Too many people readily accept defeat—they hang their heads and look for excuses. But God wants you to hold up your head and claim the victory in His name.

A third lesson is learning how to *tap your inner strength.* Your body has many muscles, but if you do not use them they become weak. Similarly, you have "spiritual muscles" that grow stronger every time they are used. You do not need to be seven feet tall in order to stand head and shoulders above those around you. David was not a large physical specimen, but he killed a giant because his spiritual muscles were equal to the task. Unlike physical strength, spiritual strength cannot be measured, for it comes from God and is without limit. It is the quality of your life that makes the difference, and the power of choice is yours. By choosing to exercise your spiritual muscles, you can grow in stature as Jesus did.

The fourth lesson in learning to stand tall is realizing that *you hold the key to your own destiny*. It may seem that you do not, that someone else controls your fate besides yourself, but this is an illusion. You may tend to blame others for your failures instead of accepting responsibility for them. You may blame your parents, your employer, or your spouse for your unhappiness, but in truth you have chosen to be unhappy and you can choose differently. You are the one in control of your life, and you can choose to give it to God and serve the Lord. God wants you to succeed and to find fulfillment, and to do this you must take hold of your own destiny. You can dissipate your life in sin and shrink yourself into nothing, or you can make a new beginning and resolve to stand tall before God and humanity. Make good things great and great things greater in Jesus' name.

The fifth lesson is that *you must stand tall alone*. Stand up for yourself; speak for yourself; assert yourself; and claim your reward. No one else can do it. It is unwise to rely on others to push you to succeed; for even if you do accomplish your goals, you will not have the satisfaction of personal success. You can go to school and have your professors help you; you can go to church and have your pastor help you; you can go home and have your family help you. But in the final analysis, you must stand tall by yourself, and this requires an individual, solitary commitment that no one else can provide. In making the commitment to yourself, you will become the great one, the strong one, the resourceful one, the creative one, and you *will stand tall!* Not only will you gain the respect of others, but you also will glorify God and gain personal satisfaction and peace.

Why Stand Tall?

You may ask, "Why should I stand tall?" There are several reasons. First, we find in Genesis 1:26 that God gave humanity dominion over the earth. We were created tall, but we have diminished ourselves by sin. God made us to stand tall, and those people who do are closer to God's plan and therefore closer to God. Furthermore, God ordained that as the rulers of the earth we would rule ourselves. In order to govern ourselves effectively, we must reflect the image in which we were made and stand tall in our communities. Standing tall is a choice we can make for the good of our environment.

You must also realize that the devil hates for you to stand tall. Failing to realize this important fact can bring trouble upon you. Mary Magdalene wasn't able to stand tall until Jesus cast seven demons out of her. She stood tall at Jesus' crucifixion and again after His resurrection. By standing tall, she lives in history two thousand years later, but if she had remained a slave to Satan, she would have been forgotten immediately. The Bible says, "He who is in you is greater than he who is in the world" (1 John 4:4). If Jesus could transform Mary Magdalene into a woman of faith and courage, He can do the same for you. You may have made mistakes, you may have slipped into the gutter, but you can stand tall again by taking Jesus into your heart.

How Do I Start?

You may ask, "How can I start standing tall?" The first and most important step is to believe in yourself. If you believe you will succeed, then success can be yours. Cling to Philippians 4:13: "I can do all things through Christ who strengthens me." Sin cannot overcome you if you believe the promises of Scripture. The Lord wants you to succeed, and He will help you in your struggle to overcome sin and wrongdoing.

In Acts 1:8, Jesus told His disciples they would receive power. Do you know what power is? Power is two different things: authority and energy. On one hand, authority is the kind of power a ruler has; his word is obeyed and his opinions are heeded. Energy, on the other hand, is the kind of power that heats your home or moves your automobile. God can provide both authority and energy, and we need both to stand tall, especially today, when more people than ever before are beaten down by sin and are hurt in so many ways.

Next, you must realize that there is a time to stand tall. God has a plan for everyone and everything, and timing is important. For example, in the third chapter of Acts, Peter and John healed a lame man who had begged at the Beautiful Gate for forty years. Jesus probably had passed through the same gate a hundred times without healing the man. Why didn't Jesus heal him? We can almost hear Jesus saying to himself, "Poor man, crippled man, just a few more days. Two of my disciples, Peter and John, will come by here and will speak health and life into your bones, and five thousand men, women, and children will come into eternal life through the miracle I grant unto you." There is a time and a place for everything in God's plan, and often the best way to find God's will for you is to have the patience to wait until God is ready to move in your life.

Finally, believe above all that God is seeking you. Believing in yourself and in the timing of God's plan for you are worthless if you do not believe God wants you to stand tall and will help you. Regardless of the sin in your past life, God can and will use you to accomplish His will.

In the book of Acts, Saul was a young Roman who "made havoc of the church, entering every house, and dragging off men and women, committing them to prison" (8:3). No one would have suspected that this fearful Roman was in God's plan, but the Lord sought him, Jesus came into his heart, and Saul was transformed into a new man. We know Saul better as the apostle Paul, who spent three years reading, studying, receiving revelation, and growing spiritually. Now, two thousand years later, we name baby boys Paul after him because he was an upright and great man.

Just as God sought Paul, God seeks us to use the talents and potential He has given us. In making the most of ourselves, we glorify God, who made us and gave us our different abilities. In reaching your potential you come closer to God's plan for your life. He has made each of us for a specific purpose, but it is up to us to stand tall and take our rightful places in God's plan.

A Parable

Once upon a time there was a man who was walking in the forest. He found an abandoned baby eagle that had not learned to fly, and he took it home to care for it. He put it in the barnyard pen with his chickens, where it soon learned to eat chicken feed and to behave as a chicken behaves.

One day a neighbor was passing by the man's farm and noticed the eagle. He asked the man why an eagle, the king of birds, would live in a barnyard with chickens.

"Because I gave it chicken feed and trained it to be a chicken, it never learned to fly," said the man. "It acts like a chicken and believes it is a chicken, so it is not really an eagle anymore: it is a chicken."

The neighbor insisted the bird was still an eagle at heart and could be taught to fly. So the man agreed to allow the neighbor to test his theory. Gently he took the eagle in his arms, held it toward the sky, and encouraged it to take off. However, the eagle was confused. Not realizing its true nature, it jumped back into the pen with the chickens.

The neighbor was not dismayed by this reaction and returned the following day to try again. Once more he encouraged the eagle to stretch its wings and soar, but once more the eagle was afraid of its unknown self and returned to the chickens.

On the third day, the neighbor took the eagle away from the barnyard to the top of a mountain. There he held the majestic bird above him so that it could survey its rightful realm. Again he encouraged the eagle to fly.

The eagle was afraid and looked back toward

the ground and the barnyard. The neighbor raised the eagle even higher toward the sun, and the bird's wings began to tremble. Suddenly with a great cry the eagle spread its wings and launched itself into the heavens.

It may be that the eagle occasionally remembers its life in the barnyard with the chickens and perhaps looks back on it nostalgically. But the eagle never returned to the life of a chicken, for it was meant to be an eagle. No amount of conditioning, training, or confinement could deny the potential it was born with. Similarly, Christians are not to deny their own potential. We must learn, like the eagle, to stand tall, to claim the inheritance in Christ which is our birthright, and to fulfill our Christian potential.

6

How to Love Deeply

There is a "secret" to successful, happy living of which many people are unaware, yet it is quite simple. The secret is this: people who love deeply succeed. Do you love your job? Do you love your family? Do you love God?

Deep love is not easy to find or feel. Many people love shallowly and lose the respect and devotion of their families and friends. Many people do not know how to love deeply, yet deep love is exactly what they need most. By learning how to love deeply, they can be changed forever. In this chapter we will look at biblical examples of deep love and gain insight into what love is and what it takes to live a life of love.

Remember that God loved the world so much that He sent Jesus to forgive our sins, and Jesus loved us so much that He died on the cross for us. In John 13:35 Jesus said about love, "By this all will know that you are My disciples." We can identify disciples of Jesus Christ by their love for one another. If you believe that you are a disciple, but you do not love your neighbor, you are not recognizable as a disciple of Christ.

If it were necessary for you to sum up Christianity in one word, would you choose the word *love*?

If you were to choose another word, perhaps you are confused about the word *love* because of the many shades of meaning it can express and the frequency with which it is used. Discovering the true meaning of love is both a challenge and a commitment. The most challenging call ever issued comes from Jesus, who said, "A new commandment I give to you, that you love one another; as I have loved you" (John 13:34). Thus, the kingdom of God within each of us is a kingdom of love, not only for those who love us in return but also for strangers and enemies.

What Is Love?

According to 1 Corinthians 13, the famous love passage, love is selflessness. When we love others, we put their concerns before ours and care about their welfare before our own. Our love for one another is the truest testimony that we believe God loves us.

In his second letter to the Thessalonians, Paul wrote, "Now may the Lord direct your hearts into the love of God and into the patience of Christ" (v. 3:5). You do not come into the love of God by accident, but by listening to the Lord and allowing Him to direct your path. Christ will manifest Himself in you if you allow Him to and are patient.

There are many feelings we call "love," but true love is divine and is wholly different from friendship and from love based on desires of the flesh. It is unconditional: "We love Him because He first loved us" (1 John 4:19). We are imperfect and love imperfectly, but God loved us before we were loving Him.

The first letter of John also says, "In this is love,

not that we loved God, but that He loved us and sent His Son to be the propitiation for our sins" (4:10). What a gift of love! Having been loved so freely, shall we fail to give love in return? No, we would not want to deny our heavenly Father but would uphold John 14:15: "If you love Me, keep My commandments." His greatest commandment was to love.

Therefore, patterning ourselves after the love of Christ, we must eliminate selfishness and self-pity, the greatest barriers to love. Those who are unable to see anything but their own reflections in everyone and everything around them are too obsessed to give and to receive deep love and trust. Such people need to discover how the cross of Christ can purify their lives and make them into what God wants them to be. Living selfishly is not living: it is death in life. Hatred is not living: those who hate rather than love are already dead. You are dead inside when you hate.

Jonathan and David

One of the greatest stories of love in the Bible was that of a prince named Jonathan, a son of King Saul, for a shepherd boy named David. The Bible tells us they loved each other deeply: "Jonathan took off the robe that was on him and gave it to David, with his armor, even to his sword and his bow and his belt" (1 Sam. 18:4). The crown prince of Israel gave his princely garb to David when David needed it. King Saul had become jealous of David's popularity with the people of Israel and feared (correctly) that David would take his throne. Saul's son and heir apparent logically should have been jealous of David as well, yet Jonathan supported David and was not envious or jealous of him at all. Jonathan had bowed to God's will: his attitude indicated that if God wanted David to be king, then Jonathan wanted David to be king also.

The Bible says in 1 Samuel 18:1, "It was so, when he had finished speaking to Saul, that the soul of Jonathan was knit to the soul of David, and Jonathan loved him as his own soul." Jonathan was nobly born, yet his high station did not prevent him from becoming a true friend to a shepherd. One lesson we learn from this is that outward distinctions and worldly concerns have no meaning in the kingdom of God: all men are brothers, and all are equal in God's sight.

We also learn from Jonathan and David that those who are weak can never love deeply, for often love requires courage. It took great amounts of courage for Jonathan to persist in his love for David in the face of Saul's jealousy. Just as Jonathan disregarded his safety for his loyalty to David, so must we place such a high priority on our love for others.

Ruth

Another great love story is found in the book of Ruth. Ruth was a pagan woman who had the good fortune to marry into a family who worshiped the living God, and Ruth adopted her new family's ways. Shortly after her marriage, Ruth's husband died, whereupon her new mother-in-law tried to send her back to her own people and her own gods. Most people would probably follow such advice under the circumstances, but Ruth's reaction was unusual: "Ruth said, 'Entreat me not to leave you, or to turn back from following after you; for wherever you go, I will go'" (Ruth 1:16). It was not easy for Ruth to risk moving to a foreign land, especially one that most likely would not welcome her because of her religious background, but Ruth's love for her mother-in-law and for the one true God superseded her fear. Ruth, too, was courageous in order to love deeply.

When her mother-in-law saw that Ruth was steadfast and intended to accompany her, she relented and allowed her to do so. Ruth eventually remarried, and through her descendants the Messiah was born. Thus a pagan, a disbeliever, was brought into the family of God through her deep love of God and family, and became part of the royal lineage of the King.

How to Love

Have you ever met anyone for whom you would gladly sacrifice your life? This is what Jesus did for humanity, and as Christians, we must feel the same sacrificial love. John 15:13 says, "Greater love has no one than this, than to lay down one's life for his friends." The ability and the willingness to make such a sacrifice is the true test of genuine love. In loving this deeply, we find exuberant happiness now and everlasting life hereafter. God wants us to love deeply so we can claim our reward of eternal life in heaven.

Those who want to give and receive deep love must decide whom to love and how to love. The Bible provides the answer: "Therefore love the strangers, for you were strangers in the land of Egypt" (Deut. 10:19), and "You shall love your neighbor as yourself" (Matt. 22:39). You know who your neighbor is where your work and where you live. You may not know his or her name, but it is still your responsibility as a Christian to try to know and understand your neighbor, and to love him or her no matter what happens.

Romans 12:9 says, "Let love be without hypocrisy." Too many people say "I love you" without meaning anything of the kind. Christian love, God's love, is more than lip service; it is a way of life, a whole philosophy of living. According to 1 Peter 1:22, to love our brethren with unfeigned love: "Since you have purified your souls in obeying the truth through the Spirit in sincere love of the brethren, love one another fervently with a pure heart." Our love is worthless unless it is sincere.

Paul closed his letter to the Ephesians with, "Grace be with all those who love our Lord Jesus Christ in sincerity" (6:24). This, in essence, is advice not to lie either to ourselves or to God, and we lie to Him when we fail to manifest love: "If someone says, 'I love God,' and hates his brother, he is a liar" (1 John 4:20).

Faith Equals Love

Galatians 5:6 affirms that faith works through love. Many people believe that faith works miracles or that faith will make them rich in material goods. However, the Bible tells us that the essence of faith in God is loving God, so that when we begin to love we also begin to have faith. Faith and love flow together. Ephesians 3:17 says we are "rooted and grounded in love." Christians draw spiritual strength and nourishment from God's love just as a plant draws nutrients from the ground through its roots. God's love is the Christian's foundation; the Christian is rooted in love from the innermost part of his or her being.

Deep within each of us, we are all committed to some cause, some ideal, some goal. The Christian's goal is to be as much like Jesus as possible, and this means caring for others. We have no finer example of love than Jesus' life which was a continual ministry to others, and His death was the sacrifice of perfect love.

"Put on love, which is the bond of perfection" (Col. 3:14) was Paul's advice to those who seek God's perfect love. The law of perfection is to "put on love," or to begin with the love that leads to faith and ends in heaven. God's love is always available to those who seek it. If you do not know God's love, it can be yours any time—all you have to do is ask God's forgiveness for your sins and seek His will for your life.

Human existence is meaningless without deep love. Many people have walked across life's stage without loving anyone or anything deeply, and as a result they have never known God's available love. God showers His blessings upon those who love Him deeply. He requires of His people the ability to love deeply and to base their lives on deep love for God, for others, and for themselves.

The Challenge of Love

Christian love is more than a topic to be studied or a concept to be understood. It demands action from each and every believer. Love must be something we do actively if it is going to make a difference in how we live.

Our first and greatest challenge in practicing love for others is to widen the circles of people who receive our compassion and concern. This process must be done in a nondiscriminating manner if it is to be effective: God's people must love their neighbors as they love themselves and also must love their enemies.

Who is your neighbor? According to the story of the Good Samaritan, a neighbor is anyone who is in need. And to Jesus, everyone is in need. Jesus came under sharp criticism because He associated with sinners, yet He was love personified. He demonstrated a depth of love that reached beyond His immediate surroundings to include the lost and the lonely.

Jesus' greatest challenge to us is to love our enemies. It is difficult enough to love our friends and families selflessly, but to love those who do not return our love seems unnatural to us imperfect lovers. Nevertheless, Jesus' commandment is clear:

> There is a saying, "Love your friends and hate your enemies." But I say: Love your enemies! Pray for those who persecute you! In that way you will be acting as true sons of your Father in heaven. For he gives his sunlight to both the evil and the good, and sends rain on the just and the unjust too. If you love only those who love you, what good is that? Even scoundrels do that much. If you are friendly only to your friends, how are you different from anyone else? Even the heathen do that. (Matt. 5:43–47 TLB)

The most natural thing to do is to retaliate

against our enemies, but Jesus instructs otherwise. Maintaining a positive attitude toward those who oppose us is a virtue we must constantly learn and relearn, just as retaliation is a tendency we must resist.

In seeking to obey Jesus' commandment, you may not know how to begin to love your enemies. There are four important ingredients in the recipe for finding this kind of love for others within ourselves. First, remember that God loves all people, not just you and your friends. If someone differs from you in any way, that difference does not affect God's love at all, and to think otherwise is a dangerous self-deception.

Second, remember that you personally may not be the target of the other person's hostility. Someone may only be "blowing off steam" in your direction since you happen to be a convenient substitute for the real target.

Third, pray for your enemies, even if you don't want to or don't feel like it. Most people who cannot pray for their enemies are unable to forgive them. But Jesus taught that "If you do not forgive men their trespasses, neither will your Father forgive your trespasses" (Matt. 6:15).

Fourth, continue to pray for your enemies until you have eliminated your hostility toward them. It is necessary not only "formally" to forgive others on each occasion they offend you, it is also necessary "informally" to forgive their actions each time they surface in your memory. The thought of past wrongs perpetrated against you eventually will neither dominate your thoughts nor prevent you from expressing love for those who do you wrong. Christian love turns the other cheek, goes the extra mile, and excludes no one.

7

How to Live in Times Like These

When we pause to think upon the times in which we live, it is important to remember the nature of the period in which we find ourselves. We are daily seeing prophecy being fulfilled at an alarming rate. The predictions made in the Old Testament in Daniel and in other books are coming true with an accuracy that speaks strongly of the Spirit of God.

Daniel 12:4 predicts that "knowledge shall increase." This is certainly true these days with the accelerated progress in technology and computer science. By contrast, sixty years ago life moved at a much slower pace: cars had to be cranked, refrigerators used ice, and washboards rather than washing machines were in widespread use.

Read the Times

It is clear that, during this century, humanity's knowledge of itself and of the world have increased faster than ever before. Let's look back for a moment over the past decades to see how our current situation evolved from previous ones.

The so-called Roaring Twenties was generally

considered to be a prosperous time in America. Lifestyles changed, notorious killers were on the loose, and new dances appeared often. The 1930s was the time of the Great Depression. Many people were out of work, and still more had no money or means of survival. Economically, the country was at its lowest ebb ever.

The 1940s brought World War II and Hitler, and with the war came economic recovery. The "Golden Age of America" was the 1950s, when we had prosperous times and good government, yet all the same a war was brewing in Korea. War continued into the 1960s with the conflict in Vietnam, and during these years many Americans began to express discontent with the seemingly endless series of American military actions.

Unrest from previous years was forgotten in the 1970s, when our country went to the moon and began to provide for the underprivileged. Still, great violence swept America during these years.

We are now midway through the 1980s, and violence and crime are on the rise. In addition, the world hovers dangerously near the brink of nuclear devastation. Could the next few years be the ones spoken of by Ezekiel, Daniel, and Jeremiah in their prophecies?

Christians have been planting "spiritual seed" for the last few years, and soon will come the harvest. We can look forward to the greatest outpouring of God's love we have ever known. This outpouring of the Spirit will reach such a height that it could possibly herald the Rapture of the church. We are seeing an increasing spiritual awareness in our time, but we also see darkness, gloom, despair, war, famine, and earthquakes, as predicted by the Lord Jesus Christ. Any intelligent person who contemplates these facts realizes that the world's chaotic condition cannot endure much longer, and that a major upheaval is imminent.

Live in Him

Jesus speaks to us concerning these times in Matthew 24, Mark 13, and Luke 21. Luke 21:28 tells us, "Now when these things begin to happen, look up and lift up your heads, because your redemption draws near." Therefore, we should have an attitude of joyous expectancy rather than one of complacency and apathy, because the coming of the Lord is near. At such times, our task is to turn people to righteousness and let them see by word and deed how to face life's problems. Christians are to be good examples and should avoid becoming part of the problem, as did Lot who lived in Sodom. Compromising ourselves by joining disbelievers during a crisis is like riding on a train with no brakes: sooner or later tragedy will strike, and we will regret our rash abandonment of God at the time we need Him most.

Speaking of the last days, the apostle Peter has recorded this admonition:

> Therefore humble yourselves under the mighty hand of God, that He may exalt you in due time, casting all your care upon Him, for He cares for you.

> Be sober, be vigilant; because your adversary the devil walks about like a roaring lion seeking whom he may devour. Resist him, steadfast in the faith, knowing that the same sufferings are experienced by your brotherhood in the world. (1 Pet. 5:6–9)

Timothy, Paul's understudy, spoke of the last days as follows:

> But know this, that in the last days perilous times will come: For men will be lovers of themselves, lovers of money, boasters, proud, blasphemers, disobedient to parents, unthankful, unholy, unloving, unforgiving, slanderers, without self-control, brutal, despisers of good, traitors, headstrong, haughty, lovers of pleasure rather than lovers of God, having a form of godliness but denying its power. And from such people turn away! (2 Tim. 3:1–5)

Because of such prophecies, Christians have the "inside track" on the future. The church needs to inform the world of the good news and reform the world by the Word of God. The process of receiving the Word will turn the world's darkness into light.

The Bible states that we, God's children, are not children of darkness but are illuminated by truth. We have many wonderful opportunities each day to reach out to the world with the gospel, the good news, of Jesus Christ. When you meet a person who is bound and fettered by habits, lust, and perversion, and is driven by an unseen force, then you can proclaim liberty to him by telling him the good news of Jesus.

Reach Out

By means of technological advances in the media—in print, radio, television, satellite communications, and in the rapidly growing computer industry—numerous powerful tools are available today to spread the gospel of peace. Such an opportunity is unique in the history of Christianity, and today's Christians no doubt will be held accountable for their opportunities to share in world evangelism. Television alone opens a vast door to masses of people who would be almost impossible to reach in other ways. I believe that if the apostle Paul were alive in this century, he would make use of media. His powerful dialogues and sermons, communicated via radio and television, would shake thousands by the power of God surging through him.

In addition, Christians today have superior means of transportation and therefore greater and more numerous opportunities to travel and spread the gospel. The Lord's Great Commission is still in effect: "Go into all the world and preach the gospel to every creature" (Mark 16:15).

Humanity is searching today as never before for the supernatural. It seems that human beings have a natural desire to find a *higher power* to resolve the question of life's meaning and purpose. They always involve themselves in worship of one type or another and if they do not find their answers in religion, they may turn to occult practices or to cult groups. Today's Christians must show the people of our generation that God is alive and that He rewards those who seek Him.

There are more cults today than ever before because more people than ever before are seeking to know the unknown, to see the unseen, and to understand that which exists in another, higher dimension. In addition, many people are obsessed by various kinds of recreational pastimes into which they pour the energy that would otherwise be spent doing God's will. For example, billions of dollars are spent each year to keep vast numbers of people amused with sporting events. There is at least one sport for each season of the year: golf, basketball, tennis, baseball, football, and hockey are all multimillion dollar enterprises that dominate not only the various communications media but people's minds as well. All these substitutes can never take the place of God in their lives. Try as they will, they never can come to God without being drawn by the Spirit.

In the analysis of how to live in times like these, let us affirm that our day and age is the time of prophecy spoken of by the prophets and the apostles. Our task is to see our time as the last days of God's glory manifested through His people so that the world will see, magnify, and worship God for what He has done. Great reservoirs of blessings are about to engulf us and to usher in the days of victory and triumph, of sights and miraculous visitations by God, and the spiritual harvest is about to begin: "Therefore be patient, brethren, until the coming of the Lord. See how the farmer waits for the precious fruit of the earth, waiting patiently for it until it receives the early and latter rain" (James 5:7).

Notice the reference to early and latter rain, which speaks to us about revival and about the spiritual outpouring to come. Now is the time to let the deluge from heaven rain upon us in glory and to advance the kingdom of God to which we look with great anticipation.

Jesus affirmed that the kingdom of God grows when people who have experienced it share with those who have not. Witnessing is a vital part of our mission on earth. We need to know not only how to witness but also how to commit ourselves to do it. Our realization of what it means for people to be lost is very important, for this provides a large part of our motivation to spread the gospel. Let's consider in turn both the *will to witness* and the *skill to witness*.

The Will to Witness

Our will to witness can increase as we become more aware of ourselves and of the internal blocks that prevent us from witnessing effectively. Few are immune from at least one of these stumbling blocks, and most people experience them all at some time or another during witnessing. Knowing how and why we are likely to have difficulty witnessing can prepare us to do our best, even under hostile conditions.

A major obstacle to effective witnessing is the fear of ridicule. In the years following Jesus' resurrection, Christians were severely persecuted, yet Peter and John found the courage to carry on their ministry. Fortunately, citizens of the United States are not prohibited by law from sharing their faith; however, they are not immune from other threats. The persistent threat of ridicule and intimidation is a common difficulty for many believers. They should remember that Jesus was often ridiculed and criticized, but He paid his persecutors no heed.

Perhaps you are a timid person, and speaking to people about deep personal matters such as religious beliefs is quite difficult for you to do. You may be surprised to discover how many people will hear you gladly. Remember that our motivation for witnessing is based on the words of the Savior: "You shall be witnesses to Me" (Acts 1:8).

A second potential obstacle to witnessing is the feeling of inadequacy for the task. Human beings are far from perfect, and they often make errors in judgment. Many Christians fear that people will not accept their testimonies as valid because they still commit sins as Christians. The solution to this dilemma is for Christians to realize they are not perfect and are in need of God's grace and forgiveness. When they admit their fallibility, they become less vulnerable to criticism and more effective in their ministries.

A third obstacle to effective witnessing is the fear of being ineffective. Such a fear arises from lack of skill. Since skillful witnessing comes from practice, there is no way to avoid risking failure. We can take comfort in the certainty that the Holy Spirit is present whenever and wherever we witness and that our task is simply to be faithful to Christ.

The Skill to Witness

No one improves his or her skill in any area without considerable practice, and witnessing is no exception. However, just making the effort to witness improves one's ability to do so. There are three basic ways to witness: through personal testimony, through Bible study, and through acts of ministry. Any individual instance of witnessing may consist of any combination of these methods.

One way to witness is to share our personal stories of what God has done and is doing in our lives. This kind of testimony is effective for several reasons. It is authoritative since it arises from the unique circumstances in our lives. It is interesting since in witnessing we are also sharing ourselves with others. Finally, it is something virtually all believers can do. Through practice, we can come to speak about our deepest religious experiences with the same ease with which we discuss other topics. Our testimonies can be about how we became Christians, but they also can be about God's presence in our day-to-day affairs as well.

A second witnessing skill is knowing how to use the Bible. The Scriptures were used freely by early Christians to proclaim that Jesus Christ fulfilled many Old Testament prophecies. As a modern Christian, you do not need to be a Bible scholar to use the Bible as a witnessing tool; knowing a few passages is usually quite adequate. Your pastor and your fellow Christians will have suggestions.

The third and final skill in witnessing is the most common one: witnessing through acts of ministry. Benevolent actions demonstrate that we really care about others, and as a result they may be more inclined to be attentive to our message. Performing acts of charity in our ministry opens lines of communication through which the message of salvation can travel.

One of the true tests of a Christian's relationship with God is his ability to share his faith with another person. Witnessing is a challenge, but it helps the believer maintain a vital relationship with Christ and grow in the Spirit. Consistent witnessing promotes Christian growth and knowledge, and it enables us to become all that God intends for us to be.

8

How to Be Fulfilled

Daydreaming is a normal activity. In the never-never land in your mind there is no pain, no strife, no financial woe. In the privacy of your mind you can go to the lush gardens of Hawaii or can circle the world on a cruise ship. You may dream of having peace of mind or of having a joyous heart. Sadly enough, peace of mind and joy of heart are so distant to many people that they seem like impossible dreams.

Begin Now

The reason Christians often feel fulfilled is the same reason that the Bible is relevant to modern living: they can attain all their hopes, dreams, and plans without having to wait for the elusive "some day" that never arrives for most people. Many Scriptures speak about the immediate fulfillment of dreams. The Bible tells us that "now is the accepted time; behold, now is the day of salvation" (2 Cor. 6:2).

Nothing starts without salvation; it is the logical and best place to start your personal plan for fulfillment. Salvation occurs when Jesus Christ takes sin out of your life and forgives you. He removes remorse from you and forgets that you have ever sinned because you are covered by the blood He shed on Calvary two thousand years ago. Also, Jesus said in Mark 11:23 that "whoever says to this mountain, 'Be removed and be cast into the sea,' and does not doubt in his heart,...will have whatever he says."

Many of us never realize our dreams for tomorrow because we do not really believe they will come true. This disbelief in ourselves kills whatever chance we would otherwise have of achieving our goals. But Christians who truly believe can do all things, even move mountains, by the strength of their faith.

A natural question to ask about all the wonderful promises in the Bible is "Does it last?" Well, have a look at the world around you: nothing worldly lasts very long. The thrill of winning at sports or of making a successful business deal lasts a few hours and then fades; new cars last a few years and then deteriorate. Anything the world has to offer has a time limit on our enjoyment of it.

John 15:7 tells us of the relationship we have with Jesus Christ, the source of our life and strength: "If you abide in Me, and My words abide in you, you will ask what you desire, and it shall be done for you." The key to this passage is in Jesus' words abiding in us, or simply, living in us. We can attain any goal simply by asking God's help in reaching it if Jesus has come into our lives. If our goal is to feel secure, to have peace of mind and a joyous heart, then Jesus must be our source of strength.

Living under God's Shadow

Psalm 91:1–2 tells us that we can live under the shadow of the Almighty. We are not hiding when we are under God's shadow: rather, we are finding strength and protection there. By living in God's shadow, by keeping His commandments and striving to know Him, we stand closer to Him than ever before. The book of Ephesians tells us that we wrestle not against flesh and blood but against powers and principalities and rulers of evil forces (see 6:12). When we live in the shadow of the Almighty, we are standing on high ground, and there is no battle we cannot win.

Believers in Jesus have a source of strength that nonbelievers often envy. Secure in knowing the solution to life's problems, Christians need not resort to skirting issues or to escaping reality as nonbelievers often do when faced by difficult decisions. Having a limitless reservoir of strength drawn from God enables Christians to have a positive attitude because they know that no problem is too difficult, no task too large, no burden too heavy to bear when it is done in Jesus' name.

The inner strength God gives to each of His children is referred to in John 4:14: "But the water that I shall give him will become in him a fountain of water springing up into everlasting life." This living water bubbles up to the surface, finding expression in a joy that makes the believer oblivious to external threats because he knows his strength and help come from above. Feeling secure is a matter of allowing this kind of joy to come into your life.

You can never run from life's problems—you

must face them head-on. Yet your own power and ability are not adequate to solve every problem that comes your way. What will you do? Will you seek refuge in the self-delusion of escapism, as many do? Or will you seek a source of strength and guidance that equips you to handle any situation?

God's strength and power are what we need most: it is very important to estabish a close relationship to God. The Almighty is omnipotent and omniscient; thus, He is never too soon or too late but is always right on time in every situation. Feeling secure is simply a matter of living in and through the power and ability of Jesus.

We are vessels of God's love, and it is love that forms the basis for the church and its ministry. Nonbelievers who look to the church are looking for the supernatural demonstration of God's love and want more than anything else to know whether or not a Christian can stand up to pressure. The answer has always been yes and always will be as long as men seek to know Him.

Command Fulfillment

Why do people quit and back off into obscurity just when it looks as if they are ready for something magnificent to happen in their lives?

In my experience, I have noticed that some of the most promising young people will rise rapidly to a certain point in their spiritual growth, then rise no more, and eventually slide backwards. Why doesn't a person's spiritual life grow onward and upward? Why doesn't life's ministry get better and better?

There would not be nearly as many people in retirement homes today if those people had done some planning long ago. If you are cantankerous when your children get married and are glad they are out of the house, you will regret your attitude in later years. If you seldom visit them and do not wish to help them when they need help (as newlyweds often do), they will reach maturity when you are in your declining years, and the roles will be reversed. They will not want to visit you because of how you behaved years ago. You may end life with your head down and your heart sad, wondering why life has treated you so harshly.

It is possible for individuals in our world today to become selfish, so much so that there is no room for children, or for parents, grandparents, and relatives. Old people are especially neglected. It is important to remember that eventually we all become old. If you complain because elderly relatives are your responsibility, remember that one day you will be old and will likely be a burden to someone yourself.

I believe that we must design our lives, just as an architect designs a building. Too many people do not design their last days. If we begin to plan early enough in life, we can take care of ourselves when we are older. The best plan is a family unit that cares for one another: the family members have no need for someone to take care of them who does not know them or love them. Living without giving thought to your final years is courting unhappiness: life is not going to work out unless you plan for it to do so.

It is important to ask yourself if you want to

spend your last days alone. Most people do not, and therefore it is necessary to make very many friends. Next to family, your friends can be the greatest source of comfort and assistance available when you are no longer self-sufficient.

It is important to be of good moral character throughout your life. Many young people who follow Jesus do not fall into sin while they are in school and struggling with their careers, but after they are successful they have trouble. A new car, a large house, a good salary, and a prestigious title can bring carelessness and sin into anyone's life. Vigilance throughout life is important. Plan to live in an upright manner, and do not be deceived by worldly gains. Let's look at some biblical examples of people who commanded fulfillment by means of careful planning.

Paul lived a very full life, and he ended his life exactly as he chose to do. His philosophy was "What things were gain to me, these I have counted loss for Christ" (Phil. 3:7). Thus, anything of worldly esteem, whether money or the recognition of men, Paul counted as nothing. His natural abilities, his intellect, his vast education, and his opportunity to know people were all as nothing to Paul in comparison with knowing Jesus Christ: "I also count all things loss for the excellence of the knowledge of Christ Jesus my Lord" (Phil. 3:8). Paul taught us to know Christ and to know the great power of His resurrection. When Christ triumphantly walked out of the grave, He rebuked religious, political, and natural law, and thus demonstrated His superiority to all three.

Reaching Your Fulfillment

In Philippians 3:12, Paul said, "Not that I have already attained, or am already perfected; but press on, that I may lay hold of that for which Christ Jesus has also laid hold of me." By this, Paul meant that God's perfect plan for him had not yet been completed. Paul was the greatest man in the New Testament, and the fact that he could do so much in his lifetime speaks eloquently of the power and scope of God's plan for our lives.

People who feel that they have "arrived," that they have reached the summits of their personal abilities and goals have a real problem. No one ever truly "arrives"; no one reaches a point where there is no room for improvement or growth. Life is ever-changing, and the future, not the past, is the measure of their true abilities. Paul declared in verse 13 of the same chapter, "Brethren, I do count not myself to have apprehended; but one thing I do, forgetting those things which are behind and reaching forward to those things which are ahead." If a person had reminded Paul of a great revival the apostle had held, Paul would have said, "That's history" and would have proceeded to organize another one elsewhere. The lesson Paul taught us is to forget those things in the past and reach for the future. We must always be planning the future rather than dwelling on the past.

Paul was a man in perpetual motion because of his orientation to the future. Paul wanted to accomplish as much as possible during his lifetime. He was not content with a few successes, and neither should we be content with our own past achievements, however spectacular they might be. Paul was not conceited about what he had done and did not brag about himself, and we should follow his example.

For Paul, the present was always in a state of becoming the future, and he saw his task as molding the future to accomplish his mission on earth. He said that he was "reaching forward to those things which are ahead" (Phil. 3:13), and in so doing he was striving for total fulfillment for the future. To emphasize his commitment Paul said, "I press toward the goal for the prize" (Phil. 3:14), just as an Olympic athlete runs for the finish line.

Personal Fulfillment

Great living is a journey, just as life is a journey from cradle to grave. The stations where you stop are as important as the ultimate destination at life's end. Great living consists of never finally arriving, but of always journeying toward a goal. We should be always traveling, always pursuing new goals, and never quitting.

Notice how satisfying it is to strive for a goal. Often the attainment of the goal, however worthwhile it may be in itself, is not as satisfying as the effort expended in reaching for it. For example, you may work hard to build your own house. Living in the house after its completion is satisfying, but the real joy comes while you are building it, not after you move in! Thus, your fulfillment is in the journey rather than in the arrival. Interestingly, the secret of personal fulfillment is in never arriving, but always being en route. Goals are important since they help you plan your journey, but joyous living comes from striving for them rather than from attaining them.

Our society holds up movie stars as examples of

successful people who have "made it big." Do you know who is the most popular movie star of all time? Mickey Mouse! No one has ever had as many fans as Mickey! A children's cartoon character has more fame than do many of the most famous actors of our time put together. This is a lesson is humility: never think that your past makes you great. It is your future and what you do with it that measure your worth as an individual and as a Christian.

A danger of resting on past achievements is that you may cease to be productive. Remember that Alexander the Great wept at age twenty-five because he had no more worlds left to conquer. We remember Alexander as a world conqueror, but what else do we remember? Very little. The person who feels, as Alexander did, that there is nothing left to accomplish is doomed to accomplish nothing more. Yet there are always new challenges, new goals, and new opportunities for those who look for them. On the inside of my Bible I have written the following: "All that I have done and all that I am doing is not nearly as great as what I desire to do for Jesus." You might want to do the same. Never stop reminding yourself that there is always more that you can do with your life than what you have done in the past or are doing now, for therein lies the secret of fulfillment.

Commanding fulfillment means becoming stronger through decision-making and through overcoming challenges. If you are satisfied with yourself as you are, you are finished. But if your spirit is reaching out, whether in the business world, in your family life, or in the spiritual realm, you are growing in the Lord. The Bible provides Moses as a good example of what we are talking about: the constant journeying that commands fulfillment.

Moses never felt that he had "arrived." He grew up in the king's palace and was considered the son of the Pharaoh's daughter. But Moses was not satisfied with the life of a monarch and chose another destiny for himself. Read the story of Moses: you will find a man who for all those forty years was reaching for God and looking for strength. Rather than becoming another in a long line of unspectacular Egyptian rulers who are best remembered as mummies, Moses chose another life.

Moses' decision was fulfilled at the top of Mount Nebo when God showed him the Promised Land. Moses was 120 years old when he achieved the goal for which he had been striving most of his life. Moses was fulfilled, just as God fulfills all those who seek His will for their lives, yet at the same time, Moses was not totally fulfilled because he was always growing spiritually, always increasing in the knowledge of God. Moses grew rapidly because he had not fulfilled his destiny. After devoting his life to bringing the people of Israel to the Promised Land, Moses himself naturally wanted to enter also, but because of earlier disobedience, God refused to permit Moses to enter Canaan.

Ultimate Fulfillment

If there is anything that is truly disturbing to see, it is a person who is living a "half life," one who believes he has arrived when in fact his goals are unreached. Such a person creates difficulties for himself because he is caught in the trap of self-delusion and is unlikely to be productive until his perception of himself becomes less fantastic.

I believe God wants all of us to reach for more and to reach further than we have ever reached before. I encourage you in Jesus' name always to be on the watch for something new, something good, something better! God has created special things for all people—it is up to you to believe in order to claim what He has in store for you.

Living dynamically means pressing forward all the time. If a person persists in being lazy, that person is going to miss most of life's rewards. Those who only do "my part" miss most of the joy that comes from serving others. Life is a miracle, and it should be treated with appropriate reverence and stewardship. It is a sin and a shame to waste a life in idleness and sloth, yet there are many people who do. On the other hand, God can do great things for those who follow Him.

Fulfillment can be lost. King David in the Old Testament was a unique person. The youngest of Jesse's seven sons, David was anointed by the prophet Samuel who had come to his father's house searching for the next king of Israel. At first David was not even introduced to the prophet, but when God did not have Samuel choose any of David's older brothers, Samuel asked if Jesse had any more sons, after which David was brought in. Samuel recognized David immediately as God's chosen one, a decision that angered David's brothers. However, David proved his superiority over them later when he faced the giant Goliath. After all the soldiers in Israel, including David's brothers, had tried to defeat Goliath, David stepped in and was equal to the task, largely because he showed no fear of the giant.

In many ways, David was as fulfilled as any believer has ever been. He had the leadership and the admiration of a nation, and he was chosen by God to fight the Lord's battles on earth. But David was human, just as we all are, and was therefore capable of error. After many years on Israel's throne, David lost his fulfillment when he did something that was completely foreign to his previous behavior. One night while strolling on his rooftop, David saw and fell in love with another man's wife and conspired to commit adultery with her.

David evidently forgot that it is possible to decrease in stature. Many successful business people make this same error, of feeling so self-important that their judgment is impaired, and as a result they make serious errors, just as David did, and deny their own fulfillment.

It is possible to be successful only in one part of your life. You may be the finest teacher at a college or university, but you may also have lost your spouse and/or children and so are unfulfilled. You may be the most capable and most knowledgeable banker in town, but if you are morally slack, all your knowledge is as nothing. The newspapers are full of stories of people who were once successful, but who were unable to maintain their success and slipped into wrongdoing. The lesson here is simple: never rest on the laurels of past accomplishments, but always reach out for something new, something better. Remember, it is possible that no human being has ever reached his or her full potential! God's strength and His provisions for you are infinite, so if you are faithful to Him, it is logical to expect that you will experience His blessings and rewards for as long as you live.

Boasting of past achievements has no place in

God's plan for you. The important thing is to stay on the right track and to keep moving. The future may be uncertain, but that's normal! Security is having faith in God's plan and His provision for you. Continue to grow and achieve. The greatest blessings you have ever known are waiting to be claimed.

Michelangelo, the famous artist, was a great example of lifelong productivity. He was already recognized in his lifetime as one of the all-time masters of painting and sculpture when at age sixty he accepted a commission from the Vatican to paint the "Last Judgment" in the Sistine Chapel. The task was a very difficult one; it required him to paint a fresco sixty feet high and thirty feet wide. It took him eight years to complete. Michelangelo was a man who would not quit, and all those who have seen the splendor of his work in the Vatican thank God that the artist kept working and accepted the challenge. Michelangelo considered his work for the Vatican the most important work he had ever done. In our work for the Lord, we should adopt a similar attitude, for there is no work that is of greater urgency.

Recall that Paul was in jail in Rome when he wrote, "All the saints greet you, but especially those who are of Caesar's household" (Phil 4:22). Paul ministered to those who were in prison with him, and he wrote letters to different churches that are still studied today as textbooks in Christian faith and philosophy. Paul was not willing to stop working and teaching until he reached heaven, and neither should we abandon our life's work before our lives on earth are ended. God will bless and fulfill a life that is devoted wholeheartedly to Him.

9

How to Move Over

If you come from a large family, you may have had to share a bed with a brother or sister. If this is the case, you very likely heard a familiar complaint at bedtime: "Move over, I don't have enough room!" There will come a time in your business or in your professional life when someone will start asking for more room as well, and it will be up to you to comply. How will you react in this situation? Will you do it God's way, the spiritual way, or will you fight to hang on? Even if you will not have to make this decision for a long time, it is never too soon to begin to think of such considerations. If you are nearing retirement age, you may already be experiencing some pressure along these lines.

This chapter's lesson is a most significant one because it is more difficult than the other lessons in this book. The topic I am referring to is the question of when and how to make the decision to move over, that is, to allow someone else, usually a younger person, to begin to assume some duties and responsibilities that you may have been doing personally for a long time.

Essentials

It is important to realize two things about moving over. First, eventually everyone is compelled to do it; second, you can make the transition between the old and the new easier by accepting this fact. Remember that, despite their fame and greatness, Nebuchadnezzar no longer rules Babylon, nor does Charlemagne rule France. We all must step aside at the proper time; we all move over some day.

To a large extent, life is composed of nothing but transitions. As we discussed in Chapter 8, life is an endless journey whose chief joys come from struggling to meet significant and worthwhile goals. This explains why it is hard for many people to retire: they have found such joy and fulfillment in their work that they would rather die than stop working. God intends for all of us to be active and productive for as long as we are able to do so, for in so doing we praise Him and bring honor upon Him and upon ourselves as well. In addition, our society encourages us to be competitive, to strive always to be the best in our chosen fields, so it is doubly difficult to renounce a lifetime of gains in order to make way for the next generation.

In learning how to move over, we must have knowledge on which to base our decisions, for without knowledge our actions are random and uninformed. The first bit of knowledge necessary for moving over is knowing how the human race has come to exist and grow. Each person only has a short span of time to make his or her unique contribution to the world. Everyone dies, but his knowledge lives on in the generations that follow.

Often one person's idea is refined by later generations into something even better. Thus, if your life is to have any lasting significance on this earth, you must allow the younger generations to have their day, for in doing so you assure the continuous flow of knowledge between generations. Do not be stingy with the information and skills you have acquired throughout your life: teach them to your successors. Those who come after you face a large responsibility, and they will need all the help they can get.

In addition, moving over requires experience. A novice has no idea how to move over because he has no experience, no training, no knowledge. But you are a seasoned veteran: you know how things work in your profession, and you know what is wrong when things don't work properly. Recall that someone had to move over in order for you to take your place when you were a novice. It is up to you to do no less now that the roles are reversed.

Make Room

Once you have learned that you must move over, you must learn when and how to make room for someone else. It is difficult to share the good things you have worked so hard to gain, and it is difficult to admit to yourself that you will not always be around to run things. I have known people who even refused to make their wills; or if they did make them, they were so poorly planned that no one knew how to execute them. Then these people died, and all that was left in their wakes were tremendous squabbles about how to settle their affairs.

Recall the tragic tale of Howard Hughes, who evidently never left a will that can be proved as authentic. Many bogus wills have been produced by unscrupulous people who wanted Hughes's millions, and as a result there is no way to tell which, if any of them, is the genuine article. If Hughes had been wise and had been willing to admit his own mortality, he would have taken better care of his estate by making sure he had a legal will. Howard Hughes is one of the most tragic figures of modern times because he had no understanding at all of how to move over. It's no good asking *how much* money and property Hughes left behind, because the truth is that Hughes left it *all* behind him when he died. You will leave everything behind you when you die, also. As the saying goes, "You can't take it with you"—Hughes left everything behind because there is no other way, and this same fate will befall us all.

No doubt there are people reading this right now who are so nervous they don't know what to do. Their children are asking them to move over, and they are not sure they know how to cope with it. They have been holding on to their jobs with shaky hands because they have not learned how to let go. They may have founded companies but so what? Adam was father of the human race, but when his time came, he had to move over!

The first lesson in moving over is learning to share the wealth it has taken you a lifetime to accumulate, regardless of whether this wealth is in money, knowledge, or material possessions. Failing to share what you have acquired means that all your gains will be lost. It is paradoxical but true that in order to preserve what you have gained it is necessary to give it away, yet this has always been the case and will continue to be the proper order of things long after you are dead.

Relinquish Power

The second critical lesson in learning to move over is learning to relinquish your power and position. There is no doubt that it is extremely hard to step aside for someone who has only a fraction of your experience and savvy. You may argue that you cannot afford to share your important position with such a person. But remember that God wants you to be able to share with others and to make room for them in your life. If your journey through life is nearly complete, you do an injustice to yourself, to God, and to humanity when you are unwilling to step aside.

It is hard to share your space with a newcomer. You may say to yourself, "That's my office, my desk, my chair. I can't simply turn them over to someone else." It is not easy to hand the reigns of authority over to another after many years of faithful service. All people need a certain amount of space, and you may have become accustomed to having large amounts of it to yourself because you are in an important position. Also, there is probably a small voice inside you that cries out, "But I don't want to move over!"

Remember that there is a time for everything in God's plan. It is certainly not God's plan for you to move over before your time, for such a move would profit no one. Ultimately, you are the only one who decides when the time to move over has arrived. Allow no one to rush you or to pressure you—the decision to move over is one of the last great decisions human beings are required to make, and it is a decision that comes to us all sooner or later. Ask God for the spiritual resources necessary to know when the time is right, and then have the strength and integrity to do what you know to be right. You may be amazed at the results.

Some people fear that moving over implies a loss of prestige and a consequent loss of respect from their friends and families, yet experience shows that exactly the opposite is true. The person who steps aside at the proper time finds that instead of losing respect, he or she gains the admiration and respect of family, friends, and community. Don't imagine that you are the only one who has ever had to decide to make room for younger generations: everyone knows how difficult it is to do, and those who do it well are admired both for their good spirit as well as for their wisdom.

Biblical Examples

Often elderly people are so unwilling to move over that they must be forcibly evicted. This is always a sad state of affairs, both for those who are being replaced and for the ones who will carry on in their stead. Refusing to accept that aging is a natural process and part of God's plan is a poor way to finish the good job they have done throughout their lives. We have already discussed how to be of good moral character (see Chapter 5) and how to face adversity and overcome it (see Chapters 2 and 3). Now we are going to look at some biblical examples of people whose time came to move over.

Moses

Recall the sequence of events in the Old Testament in the story of Moses. God called Moses out of the desert to lead more than two million Israelites out of Egypt. It seemed Moses would also lead Israel into the Promised Land, but God had a different plan. What a shock and a disappointment it must have been to Moses, who had led Israel across the wilderness for the past forty years, to receive instructions from God to anoint Joshua as Israel's leader into Canaan. Moses had done his job well and had completed his God-given task, and Moses no doubt wanted to enter the Promised Land and witness Israel's mighty battles there. However, Moses was not called to this task. He had to move over so that Joshua could fulfill his own destiny and thereby make Israel into a mighty nation.

Moses' reaction to the news that it was time for him to move over is an excellent example of having the proper spirit under the circumstances. Moses called all the people together and announced that he was transferring all his authority to Joshua, and he instructed Israel to follow Joshua into Canaan just as they had followed Moses into the wilderness for the past four decades. Moses then walked to the top of a mountain to look upon the land of promise that he could not enter. While Moses was on the summit looking down at the trees, fruit, hills, and valleys of the Promised

Land, God came and took Moses to heaven. Thus, Moses moved over in favor of Joshua just at the right moment and as a result received a great blessing. Moving over as Moses did made this kind of reward possible.

Elijah

Elijah was probably not an old man when God instructed him to anoint Elisha his successor as Israel's ordained prophet. Always dutiful and obedient to the will of God, Elijah sought out Elisha and anointed him. Elijah and Elisha probably traveled together for many years, during which the younger man undoubtedly learned much about the work into which he had been called. Elijah's attitude during this process was admirable. Instead of being jealous of Elisha, he was willing to take it upon himself to teach and train him, so that everything Elijah had learned during his life would not be wasted and God's work would continue through Elisha. In contrast to the sudden transference of authority from Moses to Joshua, the transition between Elijah and Elisha was a gradual one. Their example shows clearly that God's plan not only accomplishes His will but also takes human needs into account.

When the time came for Elijah to make the final move, Elisha declared that he would not leave his teacher's side regardless of the consequences. Elijah asked Elisha if he had a final request from his teacher. Elisha's answer must have startled the older man, for he asked to receive a double portion of Elijah's spirit. This request, typical of youth, was ambitious, arrogant, even brash, yet it was also granted. The lesson here is obvious: gradual transition, combined with learning and a spirit of cooperation, can multiply God's blessing in your life. Notice also that Elisha was willing to wait for the proper time to assume the mantle of responsibility and to serve as Elijah's apprentice. There is much for both old and young to learn from Elijah and Elisha.

Isaac

Moving over can also occur in a family setting. Isaac called all his sons before him and announced that he was moving over in favor of Jacob. When Jacob was an old man, he called his sons before him and announced that he was moving over. Then Jacob was touched by God, and he prophesied about each of his twelve sons. He predicted how the spirit and nature of each would develop, what kind of person each would become, and what God would do for each of them in the future.

Isaac and Jacob both realized that their leaving would not mean the deterioration of the family; rather, they demonstrated greatness of spirit when they relinquished their patriarchal authority in a graceful and timely manner. Both had enough faith in God's plan to know He would care and provide for the generations to follow, and they had enough faith in the next generation to pass the responsibility of obedience to God on to them. Family leadership inevitably must change, and in many ways it is the most important kind of change because it involves spiritual leadership as well as practical decision making.

Sometimes parents find it difficult to allow their

sons and daughters to become independent adults. This can be especially difficult when children marry and the parents are no longer responsible for them. Parents who love their children very much often find it hard to accept the fact that their children are grown and need to carry their own burdens. The time your children become adults can be joyful for you if you are willing to be less parental and more friendly. You may be surprised to discover that your children, as adults, make good friends!

It Could Be Better

Have you considered the possibility that your departure might be an asset to your company or family situation? I know it's hard to believe, but consider that by moving over you might give new dynamics to the company that it never had before. All business executives, especially old pros, have certain habits, routines, and favorite ways of doing things. After a while, these habits can narrow their vision to the point that new information and new procedures are virtually ignored in favor of tried and true methods that may be seriously out-of-date. Your business may need you to move over in order to survive. You have done a good job for a long time; the fact that the time has come to step down does not diminish your past successes at all.

Moving over can be especially difficult for pastors and for others who are called into the ministry. Many people who have served the Lord faithfully for years find it hard to accept their decreasing performance, and as a result, they refuse to consider that the Lord would be served better by new faces in their positions. This does not mean that ministers cannot continue to serve the Lord, but they may need to shoulder less responsibility than they have been accustomed to carrying. Since spreading the gospel as widely as possible is the minister's Christian call and duty, all ministers must give first consideration to spreading the Word, not to their own personal careers. This is true in moving over as it is in other aspects of the ministry, yet many ministers resist this idea.

John the Baptist said, "He [Jesus] who comes after me is preferred before me" (John 1:15). When he saw Jesus he said, "Behold! The Lamb of God who takes away the sin of the world!" (John 1:29). John the Baptist was a powerful and outspoken man who challenged kings and laypeople alike, yet when the time came for him to move over, he accepted God's will without question. That's what God wants us to do.

Moving over is the law of the earth: nations move over, empires move over, cities move over, families move over and in all earthly matters, individuals move over. There is no end to moving over in this world because nothing in this world is permanent. Only God is everlasting, and we reap our final reward when we move over for the final time into eternity with Him. By confessing our sins, we can claim our place in heaven.

Do not despise the person who fills your old job, for such an attitude makes the transition difficult for all concerned. On the other hand, no one has the right to deprive you of your right to be active and productive for as long as you choose. But you must be willing to move over because if you don't you will be pushed out of the way by the younger, more vibrant generation. You can achieve greatness by having the proper attitude when the time comes to relinquish your position of leadership in favor of a better performer. You can teach what you know—your knowledge and experience should be left behind in the move! Unfortunately, many people are not able to move over in a spirit of cooperation and wisdom. The result is that these "nonmovers" do not receive all of God's blessings available to them.

10

How to Dig Deeper

Our society is unquestionably motivated by success. When we are children, we are taught to grow up to be "somebody." When we enter as children into the kingdom of God, we naturally want to succeed as Christians. This desire takes the form of increased knowledge about the Holy Spirit, and we learn the importance of growth. Soon we discover that the process of "digging deeper" in the Spirit is a never-ending one. Our path is intended to grow brighter and brighter until the coming of our Lord Jesus Christ.

It's wonderful to watch new Christians. Their lives are overflowing with newly found love, hope, and faith—anything and everything makes them happy. Regardless of whether the choir is singing, the ushers are taking an offering, or announcements are being made, new Christians look and feel happy to be alive because they have just received a new perspective on what being alive means. Their minds and spirits are renewed, and we refer to them as "born again" because of the freshness of their outlook.

After a while, however, the newness of life in Christ wears off, and the believer may find his enthusiasm waning. He may begin noticing how much the choir sounds the same as it did last month, or that the announcements are always about the same things, or how much money he has put into the collection plate recently. Everything seems to settle into a familiar, dull pattern, and life is no longer spontaneous and joyful. At such times the believer's Christian goals may become a burdensome duty in which he finds no pleasure. His task at such times is to restore life's joy by digging deeper into faith and claiming the promise of joy in personal salvation. Often a pastor or an experienced layperson can be of invaluable assistance to him.

Set Your Goals

In America there exists the common ideal of the "American Dream," a vision that limitless success is within the reach of every individual. However, if this dream takes only monetary success into account, it will not bring wholeness, contentment, and fulfillment. In fact, a life not based on Christian values has no chance for fulfillment at all. It is important to set appropriate Christian goals throughout life. In the quest for greater spiritual knowledge, setting realistic and specific goals (see Chapter 4) is necessary. The attainment of these goals enables us to realize our Christian potential.

Realizing the potential within each of us requires a transformation of our values that begins with a personal encounter with Christ. Through Him, the transforming dream becomes a reality as we tap the new power and potential within us. Achieving deeper spiritual knowledge is similiar to a conversion experience in that we gain fresh insight and renewed vitality through a personal encounter with the Holy Spirit. Digging deeper requires that we approach our goals with no preoccupations and no fixed ideas of what we will find. The essence of deeper spiritual knowledge is God's revelation of His nature, and in order to learn we must be able to listen to what He is saying. Being receptive to His Word through prayer and Bible study requires discipline as well as faith.

Discipline Yourself

The "problem" with digging deeper is that it is neither an easy nor a popular thing to do. It is usually necessary to rearrange your personal living and thinking and living of the people close to you. Digging deeper may involve not spending every night in front of the TV set, or not attending every football game, in order to make time for prayer and for activities that promote spiritual growth.

You may find that some people whom you thought of as friends will suddenly behave as if you are almost a stranger when they detect a readjustment of your priorities. Do not be discouraged by the loss of such fair weather friends: they cannot provide the support and encouragement you need in order to grow spiritually. One of the most interesting aspects of coming closer to God is that as your faith deepens you will have less and less desire to watch TV or to attend football games. And you will find that your relationships with others will mature as you draw upon God's unlimited power.

Rely on Prayer

The surest and most effective way to dig deeper is through prayer. The Bible records numerous prayers of all kinds, from Peter's three-word prayer (see Matt. 14:30) and the publican's seven-word prayer (see Luke 18:13) to Solomon's prayer at the dedication of the Temple (see 2 Chron. 6:12–42). Everyone who has ever prayed, except Jesus, has found it difficult to define prayer. Since a detailed knowledge and practice of prayer is vital to Christian growth, let's try to answer the question: What is prayer?

One kind of prayer is an invitation to God to intervene in the midst of our needs to alleviate our distress. This kind of prayer is nothing more than giving God permission to provide aid as His love, wisdom, and power dictate. People have always brought their weaknesses and limitations to God, and He has responded by giving strength to the weak, wisdom to the foolish, help to the afflicted, and guidance to all who need it and call on His name. "Behold, I stand at the door and knock. If anyone hears My voice and opens the door, I will come in to him and dine with him, and he with Me" (Rev. 3:20).

Prayer is also work in that it demands much energy. Prayer is the noblest activity of the human soul, and it is the spiritual process whereby faith finds access to the immeasurable riches of Christ. Prayer is our effort to achieve forgiveness and new obedience. However, wise Christians do not substitute prayer for work, or vice versa. God works in answers to prayer; therefore, it falls to us to work and to pray both.

It is not surprising that through prayer we come into contact with the Almighty. What *is* surprising is that in prayer, as at no other time, we also come into contact with the powers of darkness. Satan battles for the rulership of human souls, and he despises Christian prayer. When we pray, we are fighting and thwarting Satan, and it is natural that Satan should oppose us in our efforts to pray. But prayer coupled with God's work is our most effective weapon against the prince of evil, who fears our prayers.

Prayer is many things, but most of all it is communication with heaven. It is written, "It shall come to pass that before they call, I will answer; and while they are still speaking, I will hear" (Isa. 65:24). Prayer is two-way communication. We pray in order to confess our sins and to request guidance, strength, and God's blessing, but it is important to remember that during prayer we must also take time to listen to what God is telling us. The Bible is full of examples of prayer as two-way communication. For example, the prophet Elijah spoke to God about the welfare of Israel, and God replied. Nehemiah and God conversed about the rebuilding of Jerusalem. Jesus and God spoke freely of many things.

Remember that God is not mocking you when He says, "Ask, and it will be given to you; seek, and you will find; knock, and it will be opened to you. For everyone who asks receives, and he who seeks finds, and to him who knocks it will be opened" (Luke 11:9–10). There is no doubt that God is willing to hear and to answer you when you call on Him.

Prayer is power. Just as Israel prevailed when

Moses prayed, so also do we make great victories today when we pray. Daniel was more powerful than the king because Daniel prayed. Elijah could stop and start the rain with his prayers and was also able to call fire from heaven through prayer. Paul and Silas prayed, and their jail doors were opened. Prayer is the greatest power on earth.

Prayer develops the individual's personality to the fullest. Christians are told to grow in the "grace and knowledge of our Lord and Savior Jesus Christ" (2 Pet. 3:18). Not by education and culture but by prayer do we achieve a harmonious assembly of body, mind, and spirit. Not only is prayer the best way to dig deeper into faith, it is the only way. To attempt to grow in grace by any other means is folly.

The best definition of prayer and the greatest example of effective prayer comes from Jesus, who has given us the Lord's Prayer. He prayed both in private and in public, and He prayed without ceasing. Jesus showed that prayer is, in addition to all the things we have mentioned previously, an attitude and a relation to God. Jesus' example shows us that prayer of all kinds provides the steps on our spiritual ladder to heaven. During the great crises of His life, Jesus always prayed, thus demonstrating that even when all else fails, prayer succeeds.

Rely on God

God answers our prayers if they are sincere, and He seeks to work His will through us if we truly desire to be instruments of His will. The essence of digging deeper is the establishment of a strong and vital relationship with the Almighty. Digging deeper means coming to greater knowledge of God, a lifelong task that is never truly complete since our human knowledge of God is never complete but is always growing. We must learn to rely on God and on His power to transform our lives, and this is best done when we establish a loving and trusting relationship with Him. Without such a relationship or the desire to begin one, our prayers will not be effective because they will not reflect the presence of God in our lives.

A biblical illustration of digging deeper comes from the apostle Peter, who returned to his former profession as a fisherman for a brief time after the Resurrection. He was confronted by the risen Savior, who asked, "Simon, Son of Jonah, do you love Me more than these?" (John 21:15). Peter was truly looking for a way to dig deeper into his faith and simply did not know how to do it at first. He wasn't sure how to answer the Lord he had denied allegiance to the night of His death. Jesus had told Peter that He would change Peter's life forever, and the key to understanding His promise to make Peter a fisher of men (see Matt. 4:19) is the verb *make*. Only the power of Jesus can transform us into what God wants us to be and only if we truly desire to change and to seek Him.

When we read about Peter in the Bible, we see a man whose emotions fluctuated widely, a man who had extreme joys as well as deep depressions. We get glimpses of Peter the apostle, Peter the faithful, Peter the martyr, Peter the brash, and Peter the fearful, but never do we see Peter as unrepentant or disobedient. At all times we see a man who allowed God's will to operate in his life to make him into what God intended for him to become. Peter found the secret of getting closer to the Father through His Son Jesus Christ. Because of his efforts to dig deeper, Peter's story still has an impact on humanity today, two thousand years later.

We are not as fortunate as Peter in that we will not meet Christ face-to-face in this life, but we learn from Peter's example that He is always with us. It was necessary for Jesus to appear to Peter after His death to renew the relationship between God and humanity that Jesus' ministry had founded. It is our task as Christians to perpetuate this relationship as an integral and active part of our everyday living until our Lord comes again.